Dreaming: A Very Short Introduction

Titles in the series include the following:

AFRICAN HISTORY John Parker and
  Richard Rathbone
AMERICAN HISTORY Paul S. Boyer
AMERICAN LEGAL HISTORY
  G. Edward White
AMERICAN POLITICAL PARTIES
  AND ELECTIONS L. Sandy Maisel
AMERICAN POLITICS
  Richard M. Valelly
AMERICAN SLAVERY
  Heather Andrea Williams
ANARCHISM Colin Ward
ANCIENT EGYPT Ian Shaw
ANCIENT GREECE Paul Cartledge
ANCIENT PHILOSOPHY Julia Annas
ANCIENT WARFARE Harry Sidebottom
ANGLICANISM Mark Chapman
THE ANGLO-SAXON AGE John Blair
ANIMAL RIGHTS David DeGrazia
ARCHAEOLOGY Paul Bahn
ARISTOTLE Jonathan Barnes
ART HISTORY Dana Arnold
ART THEORY Cynthia Freeland
ATHEISM Julian Baggini
THE ATMOSPHERE Paul I. Palmer
AUGUSTINE Henry Chadwick
BACTERIA Sebastian G. B. Amyes
BEAUTY Roger Scruton
THE BIBLE John Riches
BLACK HOLES Katherine Blundell
BLOOD Chris Cooper
THE BRAIN Michael O'Shea
THE BRICS Andrew F. Cooper
BRITISH POLITICS Anthony Wright

BUDDHA Michael Carrithers
BUDDHISM Damien Keown
BUDDHIST ETHICS Damien Keown
CAPITALISM James Fulcher
CATHOLICISM Gerald O'Collins
THE CELTS Barry Cunliffe
CHOICE THEORY Michael Allingham
CHRISTIANITY Linda Woodhead
CIRCADIAN RHYTHMS Russell Foster
  and Leon Kreitzman
CITIZENSHIP Richard Bellamy
CLASSICAL MYTHOLOGY
  Helen Morales
CLASSICS Mary Beard and
  John Henderson
CLIMATE CHANGE Mark Maslin
THE COLD WAR Robert McMahon
COMMUNISM Leslie Holmes
CONSCIOUSNESS Susan Blackmore
CONTEMPORARY ART
  Julian Stallabrass
COSMOLOGY Peter Coles
THE CRUSADES Christopher Tyerman
DADA AND SURREALISM
  David Hopkins
DARWIN Jonathan Howard
THE DEAD SEA SCROLLS
  Timothy Lim
DECOLONIZATION Dane Kennedy
DEMOCRACY Bernard Crick
DESIGN John Heskett
DREAMING J. Allan Hobson
DRUGS Les Iversen
THE EARTH Martin Redfern

J. Allan Hobson

DREAMING

A Very Short Introduction

OXFORD
UNIVERSITY PRESS

OXFORD
UNIVERSITY PRESS

Great Clarendon Street, Oxford OX2 6DP

Oxford University Press is a department of the University of Oxford.
It furthers the University's objective of excellence in research, scholarship,
and education by publishing worldwide in

Oxford New York

Auckland Cape Town Dar es Salaam Hong Kong Karachi Kuala Lumpur
Madrid Melbourne Mexico City Nairobi New Delhi Shanghai Taipei Toronto

With offices in

Argentina Austria Brazil Chile Czech Republic France Greece
Guatemala Hungary Italy Japan South Korea Poland Portugal
Singapore Switzerland Thailand Turkey Ukraine Vietnam

Oxford is a registered trade mark of Oxford University Press
in the UK and in certain other countries

Published in the United States
by Oxford University Press Inc., New York

British Library Cataloguing in Publication Data
Data available

Library of Congress Cataloging in Publication Data
Data available
ISBN 978-0-19-280215-6

21

Typeset by RefineCatch Ltd, Bungay, Suffolk

Printed and bound by
CPI Group (UK) Ltd, Croydon, CR0 4YY

Contents

Acknowledgements

The research upon which this book is based was conducted in the author's laboratory at the Massachusetts Mental Health Centre when it was supported by grants for the NIH, NSF, NIDA, and the John T. and Catherine D. MacArthur Foundation. I thank my colleagues for their collaboration and Nicholas Tranquillo for help with the manuscript.

List of figures

The publisher and the author apologize for any errors or omissions in the above list. If contacted they will be pleased to rectify these at the earliest opportunity.

Introduction

Dreaming has fascinated humankind since the dawn of recorded history. As dreaming is so vivid, so complex, and so emotional, it has inspired religious movements, artistic representations, and introspective scientific theories. All of these pre-modern expressions have been based on the idea that dreams contain messages that cannot be delivered in any other way.

Thus, it was thought by the early Judaeo-Christians that God communicated his intentions via certain prophets to his human subjects. This concept was the centrepiece of medieval dream theory with its postulates of the 'Gates of Horn and Ivory'. Religious reformers such as Emmanuel Swedenburg were able to meet God's angels in dreams and he thereby received instructions about founding the Church of the New Jerusalem.

Early Western artists, such as Giotto, used dreaming as a vehicle for the pictorial representation of prophetic inspiration. Sleeping saints and churchmen are shown in the same pictorial frame as the visions that their dreams inspired. In modern art, the surrealists expressed through their wild paintings the conviction that dreaming was a more authentic state of consciousness than waking. Salvador Dali, Max Ernst, and René Magritte all painted in dream language. Dali was the most surreal, Ernst the most psychoanalytic, and Magritte the most neuropsychological of these artists.

At the turn of the twentieth century, the best known of all dream investigators would be Sigmund Freud, who set out to base his theory of the mind on brain science. His knowledge of the brain was so incomplete that he was forced to abandon his famous 'Project for a Scientific Psychology', and he turned to dreaming for insights about what he construed to be the dynamic unconscious. He decided, as had all his symbolist predecessors, that dreams concealed hidden meanings elaborated as one part of the mind, and that the unconscious tried to break through the protective barrier of consciousness. Freud thus threw dream theory back to the time of Biblical scholars, Artemidorus, and other early interpreters of dreams.

This book takes up where Freud left off when he abandoned his Project. It tries to build a new dream theory on the now solid and extensive base of sleep science. To accomplish this goal, I have given a concise summary of the findings of basic brain research, sleep lab studies, and recent clinical studies of sleep and dreams. Throughout the book, I use examples taken from my own dream journal to illustrate how our new theory of dreams, called activation–synthesis, can be used to explain in physiological terms universal dream features previously ascribed to psychodynamic factors. Once this is done, the mystery of dreaming is largely stripped away, leaving the content nakedly open to understanding without complex interpretation.

The main goal of this book is to show how a scientific theory of dreaming has been developed and strengthened over the past 50 years. In the process, the book offers the reader a unique opportunity to reconsider his or her own dream theory and, into the bargain, to learn about the fascinating discoveries of modern sleep science.

Chapter 1
What is dreaming?

What causes dreaming? Why are dreams so strange? Why are they
so hard to remember? A true science of dreaming requires a reliable
definition that can lead to the reliable identification of this state
and methods of measuring its properties. During the course of work
on the brain, which led to the suspicion that it might be brain
activation in sleep that causes dreaming, we realized that the most
scientifically useful way to define and measure dreaming was to
focus on the formal features rather than the content – by this is
meant the perceptual (how we perceive), cognitive (how we think),
and emotional (how we feel) qualities of dreaming, whatever the
details of the individual stories and scenarios might be.

The radical change in emphasis, from the analysis of content to the
analysis of form, exemplifies what scientists call a paradigm shift
(a rapid change in pattern or theory). Through a formal approach,
we found an entirely new and different way of looking at a familiar
phenomenon. Whereas previously students of dreaming had
invariably asked 'What does the dream mean?', we asked what the
mental characteristics of dreaming are that distinguish it from
waking mental activity. We are *not* saying that dream content is
unimportant, uninformative, or even uninterpretable. Indeed, we
believe that dreaming *is* all three of these things, but it is already
crystal clear that many aspects of dreaming previously thought to
be meaningful, privileged, and interpretable psychologically are the

simple reflection of the sleep-related changes in brain state that we start to detail in Chapter 3.

To provide a firmer grasp of the distinction between form and content, I offer an example, taken at random from my own dream journal, which is one of hundreds that I have recorded over the years. To give a complete sense of how my journal reads and to allow the reader to compare his or her own notes on dreaming with mine I quote the entry in full. I know that you will dream of subjects quite different from mine, but I suspect that the form of your dreams is similar.

10/5/1987 En route to New Orleans for a debate on dreams at the American Psychiatric Association's annual meeting: Two nights ago, a dream of Richard Newland

It is a house maintenance nightmare. I have too much property to maintain. Richard and a friend are 'helping' me but it is an uncertain alliance, with the twin threats of incompetence and inattentiveness.

There are several scenes all with the same emotional theme: anxiety about maintenance details.

In one scene we are walking along in hilly country, perhaps toward the house, but the destination is not clear.

Then we are in a house, not at all like mine but assumed by my dreaming brain to be mine, and Richard's friend is spray painting the white wall (we have none in our house) with blue paint (neither do we have any blue rooms). The paint sprayer is a tank device of the type used to apply copper sulphate to grapevines or to exterminate cockroaches. Suddenly, the paint is being sprayed not only on the wall but upon a painting hanging on the wall.

My fears are confirmed. I yell at Richard to bid his friend stop.

For some reason, he has to go upstairs to turn off the machine (although it appears to be fully portable and self-contained) and this takes an inordinate length of time as the painting continues to suffer.

There follows a long dialogue with Richard who, while retaining continuous identity as Richard, changes physiognomy repeatedly.

His face changed as follows: a gnome-like Napoleon Carter with a cherubic sun-burned face; a wry smile and a Chinese coolie-type hat; a calf face – as in A Midsummer Night's Dream *(the ad for which did not include the calf!); and as far as I can tell, never included Richard!*

I can't remember other faces or other action from this long episode.

Before discussing the distinctions of form against content that this dream so clearly illustrates, I should comment on the circumstances of its recording and the timing of its occurrence. I was on an aeroplane, where I do a great deal of my journal writing. I was flying to New Orleans for a highly publicized and well-attended public debate on dreaming. I usually record dreams on the morning after their occurrence. The fact that I waited two days in this case probably resulted in loss of detail. But, as I will presently show, there is more than enough detail to make clear the distinction between dream form and dream content.

As far as the *content* is concerned, the dream is about my concerns for the upkeep of my farm in northern Vermont, which I have owned since 1965. Richard Newland is the son of my farmer neighbour, Marshall Newland, with whom I have had a long and complicated but successful and gratifying relationship. In spite of

3

widely divergent priorities we have managed to get along and to help each other.

For me, the meaning of the dream is transparent: I am anxious about my property and about entrusting it to people who are careless about their own houses. This characteristic, known in psychological terms as emotional salience (or relevance), is all I need to understand the dream, which is a variant on the theme of incomplete arrangements that is so recurrent in my dreams and in those of most of my friends. For reasons that I discuss more fully in Chapter 2, I see no need and no justification for treating this dream as a disguised, symbolic expression of anxiety about other related themes (my wife's interest in another Vermont neighbour, for example). While admitting that it could be appropriate and more useful to notice such an association, it does not help in understanding what caused this dream, determined its comical bizarreness, and made it so hard to remember.

Form as opposed to content

To answer the questions about causes and characteristics of dreams, it is helpful to take a formal analytical approach.

As is typical of most dreams, I am so involved in the scenario that it never occurs to me that I am dreaming. As I see Richard Newland (and his unidentified friend), see my house (even though it is clearly not mine), see the blue paint as it is sprayed on the walls, and move through the sequence of scenes, I accept all of these unlikely features as real on the strength of my hallucinatory perceptions, my delusional beliefs about them, and my very strong feelings of anxiety and apprehension.

What this means is that our sense of psychological reality – whether normal dreaming or a psychotic symptom – is set by the strength of percepts and feelings as well as by our thoughts about them. Internally generated perceptions and emotions are two formal features of dreams and they are cardinal features. To explain their intensity (compared with waking), we might expect to find that parts of the brain that generate emotions and related percepts are selectively activated in sleep. We see in Chapter 5 that this is precisely what happens!

My Richard Newland dream is not simply perceptually vivid and emotionally salient, it is also cognitively bizarre, by which I mean that, despite the persistence of the main themes, there is a flagrant disregard for the constancies of time, place, and person. Notice that Richard's friend is not identified; notice also that the house that is supposed to be mine could not possibly be so; and notice that the scenes – however poorly recalled and described – meld into one another: first we are outside walking, then inside painting. Notice, most of all, that Richard's face assumes a series of non-Richard features without ever challenging either the assumption that he is Richard, or that I am not awake but dreaming, as even a glimmer of self-reflective awareness would declare me to be.

These are the cardinal cognitive features of dreaming: loss of awareness of self (self-reflective awareness); loss of orientational stability; loss of directed thought; reduction in logical reasoning; and, last but not least, poor memory both within and after the dream. The fact that the incongruities and discontinuities of my Richard Newland dream are connected by association does not explain the looseness of those associations. Thus, it is true that the unusual spray-painting device resembles an agricultural tool; it is also true that Richard's transformed face is, first, that of another Vermont farmer neighbour, Napoleon Carter, and later a calf (Richard and his dairy farmer father, Marshall, had many calves); and it is remarkably true that Shakespeare himself celebrated the transformation of characters – turning them into each other and even into animals – in *A Midsummer Night's Dream*.

What causes the processing of such extreme associations (hyperassociative processing)? Freud, like his followers, religiously

5

believed that dream bizarreness was a psychological defence against an unacceptable unconscious wish. This seemed unlikely to many people in 1900. At the beginning of the twenty-first century, it seems impossible to us.

Just as we expect (and find) selective activation of brain circuits underlying emotion and related percepts in rapid eye movement (REM) sleep, so we seek (and find) selective *in*activation of brain circuits – and chemicals – underlying memory, directed thought, self-reflective awareness, and logical reasoning.

You may be more or less pleased by the story. You might prefer to believe that your dreams are secret messages of personal portent. But whether you like the story or not, you must surely be as dismayed as we were to realize that we did not really need brain research to take this formal approach to dreaming. Common sense alone should have dictated at least that form and content were complementary. The distinction is made with ease in other fields: consider linguistics, where grammar and syntax are complementary; consider poetry, where meter and verse enhance one another; and consider the visual arts, where genre and subject matter interact for strong effect. So, why not the domain of mental life itself? Why not in dreams? Isn't the form of dreams an important contributor to content?

As shown in Chapter 2, some brave souls did make this distinction, but their feeble voices were drowned out by the clamour of the interpreters who pandered to the deep-seated human need to believe that dreaming, as for every apparent mystery, has a deeply veiled meaning inscribed by a benevolent hand whose ways are known only to a few chosen mediators.

Dreaming and how to measure it

Let's begin our analytical odyssey by accepting the most broad, general, and indisputable definition of dreaming: mental activity occurring in sleep. But what *kinds* of mental activity occur in sleep? Many different kinds, for example:

Report 1. As soon as I fell asleep, I could *feel* myself moving just the way the sea moved our boat when I was out fishing today.

Report 2. I kept thinking about my upcoming exam and about the subject matter that it will contain. I didn't sleep well because I kept waking up and was inevitably pulled back to the same ruminations about my exam.

Report 3. I am perched on a steep mountaintop; the void falls away to the left. As the climbing party rounds the trail to the right, I am suddenly on a bicycle, which I steer through the group of climbers. It becomes clear that I make a complete circuit of the peak (at this level) by staying on the grass. There is, in fact, a manicured lawn surface continuing between the rocks and crags.

All these reports qualify as descriptions of dreaming according to our broad definition, although they are very different from one another and each is typical of the kind of sleep in which it was experienced.

Report 1 contains an internal percept, the sense of rhythmic movement imparted by the sea to a boat and to those on board the boat. This report is typical of sleep-onset dreams, especially on nights following novel motor behaviour such as skiing, or boating, or even – as in Robert Frost's poem – *After Apple Picking*. The subject has been boating, and the sense of motion, which abated immediately upon putting his foot on shore, recommences at sleep onset and reproduces, exactly, the physical experience of boating. We will have more to say later about this stimulus-induced dream, especially when we look at the theme of motor learning later in the book. For now, let us emphasize how short and relatively simple this sleep-onset dream experience is. Even though it is hallucinatory, as is Report 3, it is impoverished in its brevity and its narrow scope, its lack of characters other than the dreamer, and its emotional flatness. Many sleep-onset dream reports are richer and more variegated than this one, although they are all brief and lack the elaborate plot development of Report 3.

Report 2 is limited to thinking, or what psychologists call cognition. There is no perceptual structure, and hence no hallucinatory aspect. There *is* emotion, however. The dreamer is anxious about performance on a test and this anxiety appears to drive obsessive thinking very much in the way that it might be expected to do so in waking. The thinking described is non-progressive. The dreamer doesn't even rehearse the content of the exam material in a way that might be adaptive. Accounts of rumination such as this are often given when individuals are aroused from sleep early in the night. If they are collected in a sleep lab – as described in Chapter 3 – they are associated with the low levels of brain activation that typify what we call slow wave sleep (seen on the electroencephalograph or EEG) or non-REM sleep (NREM; this refers to the lack of eye movement). Mental activity in NREM sleep later in the night, when brain activation approaches that seen in REM sleep, can assume many of the properties of Report 3.

Report 3 is a typical REM sleep report: it is animated; it is dramatic and complex; it is bizarre; it is hallucinatory; it is delusional; and it is long, about eight to ten times as long as Reports 1 and 2 (which were given in their entirety), whereas only a small excerpt of Report 3 is given here. In the rest of Report 3, there was a scene change from the mountain peak to Martha's Vineyard Island (though I was still on the same bicycle), and then to a shopping centre, a restaurant, a dance, and a meeting of faculty colleagues. The dream also exemplifies typical dream features, such as character instability, because one of my colleague's wives is seen as a blond when, in reality, she is a brunette. The sense of movement, which is continuous, becomes particularly delightful when I become practically weightless and glide along a golf fairway. At the dance there is 'a Baltic group wearing embroidered peasant garb and stamping the floor to a loud band (I can hear the drums especially).'

There is simply no comparison between the richness of Report 3 and the restrictions of Reports 1 and 2, even though Report 2 fulfils this more rigorous definition of dreaming.

Report 3 more fully illustrates a mental experience occurring in sleep, which is characterized by:

1. Rich and varied internal percepts, especially sensorimotor (movement), auditory (drums), and anti-gravitational (weightlessness) hallucinations.
2. Delusional acceptance of the wild events as real despite their extreme improbability (a bike on a mountain peak?) and physical impossibility (gliding weightless on a golf fairway?).
3. Bizarreness deriving from the discontinuity (at least six locations) and character incongruity (a blond brunette?).
4. Emotional intensity and variety (fear, elation, and exuberance).
5. Poor reasoning – I can make a complete circuit of the peak by staying on the grass!

When we think about how the very different experiences in the three dream reports were brought about, and even what they may mean, we can easily understand the first two simply in terms of brain activation that reflects, in sleep, the dreamer's previous experience (the boat trip) and concerns about the future (anxiety about an exam). In both cases, the residual brain activation of sleep onset and early night sleep is enough to reproduce faithfully a very small part of waking experience. Report 3, however, needs a much more elaborate explanation to account for its description of events, many of which never happened and never could have happened. Brain activation, which must be powerful, and highly selective, can account for some aspects – the hallucinatory imagery and the associated movements, for example. But activation cannot account for the bizarreness and the loss of logical reasoning. If brain

9

activation were global in REM sleep, we would expect orientation and cognition to improve, not deteriorate. These changes must result from something else, something that changes the whole mode of operation of the brain and the mind. As we see in Chapters 4 and 5, this change in mode is affected both chemically and by selective brain deactivation. The net effect is that, in dreaming (compared with waking), some mental functions are enhanced while others are diminished. It's as simple as that! And every bit as complicated.

Does everyone dream?

All human beings who have been studied in sleep labs have brain activation in sleep. Periods of brain activation during sleep are associated with rapid eye movements in the sleeper. These rapid eye movements give the brain-activated phase of sleep its name: REM or rapid eye movement sleep. When awakened at the time of intense clusters of rapid eye movements, 95 per cent of sleepers studied in labs report dreaming. From this evidence, it is generally assumed that everyone does, in fact, dream in sleep; any impression to the contrary is related to the difficulty recalling dreams.

If dreaming is not interrupted by awakening, it is rare to have recall. Poor or no dream recall by many people is a function of the abolition of memory during these brain-activated phases of sleep. As the chemical systems that are responsible for recent memory are completely turned off when the brain is activated during sleep, it is difficult to have recall unless an awakening occurs to restore the availability of these chemicals to the brain.

How were dream data collected?

The reports that have been presented so far are all mine. They were recorded at home or on the road in my personal journal, which now runs to 116 volumes covering the last 25 years of my life and includes over 300 dream reports. Dream reports such as these have the great advantage of being easy and inexpensive to obtain, numerous, and, to me at least, undeniably authentic. Even though I have no recall of these dreams until I read the reports, I have the reports and I see in them the striking formal features that I have emphasized in this chapter.

These reports do, however, have corresponding deficiencies, which need to be overcome if dream science is to be universally valid. To test the generality of the findings and to be sure that I wasn't just making up dreams to fit my theory, we need to have reports from many other sources and individuals, collected under very different conditions. The dream data that we have analysed before arriving at our conclusions have thus been taken from other dream journals, sleep lab reports, and home-based reports.

Other dream journals

The best dream journal that I have found is called *The Dream Journal of the Engine Man*. Its author was a railroad buff. I like it because it was recorded in the summer of 1939 (when I was only six years old) and could not therefore have been influenced by my theories. I also like it because the descriptions are so detailed and so free of interpretation. Some are even accompanied by simple but expressive drawings. To control for the fact that the Engine Man, like me, is male, we have collected journalistic reports from our female colleagues and students. All show the same robust formal differences from waking consciousness that I have emphasized here.

Sleep lab reports

Thanks to our colleagues Milton Kramer (University of Cincinnati) and John Antrobus (City College of New York), and our own sleep lab team, we have over 1,000 reports that were collected by experimentally awakening participants in studies.

We know that sleep lab awakenings change the character of the reports in at least two ways.

1. They introduce thoughts, feelings, and percepts related to the laboratory situation, but this has no effect on dream hallucinations, delusions, or bizarreness.
2. They increase recall and the naturalism of the dream recalled. For example, more positive emotion is found in post-awakening reports, indicating that we normally sleep right through our more pleasant dreams, whereas our unpleasant ones are more likely to awaken us and tilt the scales towards negative emotion.

A major disadvantage of sleep lab reports is that they are very expensive to obtain and tend to come almost exclusively from younger individuals. Students at the universities where the labs are located are easily recruited. Finally, due to expense, they tend to be limited in number of reports per participant. No one who is a sleep lab participant can yet match the 256 reports of the Engine Man, or my 300+ reports.

Home-based reports with physiological controls

With the hope of obtaining the best of both dream science worlds, we have developed the Nightcap, a home-based sleep monitor that allows us to know what state the participants were in before their reports, to compare spontaneous awakening with experimental awakening reports, to obtain abundant data from each person, and, best of all, to obtain reports in natural settings (Figure 1). Using this approach we have been able to accomplish two feats that have never before been attempted.

One is to obtain a very large number of reports from each of three

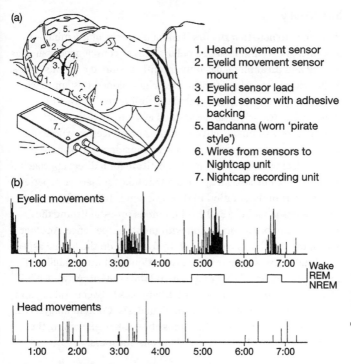

(a)

1. Head movement sensor
2. Eyelid movement sensor mount
3. Eyelid sensor lead
4. Eyelid sensor with adhesive backing
5. Bandanna (worn 'pirate style')
6. Wires from sensors to Nightcap unit
7. Nightcap recording unit

(b)

Eyelid movements

1:00 2:00 3:00 4:00 5:00 6:00 7:00

Wake
REM
NREM

Head movements

1:00 2:00 3:00 4:00 5:00 6:00 7:00

1. Line drawing made from a photograph of a subject sleeping with the Nightcap, together with Nightcap output and analysis. Top trace: histogram plot of eyelid movements; second trace: hypnogram of computer-scored Nightcap data; third trace: histogram plotting head movements.

sleep conditions: sleep onset, NREM, and REM sleep. The other is to obtain comparable reports from two states of waking by beeping the same participants with a home pager during the daytime. Thus, the same participants who give us dream reports also give us reports of their waking consciousness. This last advantage is crucial to our effort to extend our understanding of mental life back into the waking state, and to obtain comparable quantitative data from the minds of the same individuals when awake and asleep.

Summary

It is ironic to note that the first task of a science of the mind – to describe, define, and measure polar states of consciousness such as waking and dreaming – has only recently assumed a serious status. Although artists and poets have long championed this approach and have appropriately celebrated the differences between conscious states, scientists have shied away from their study because they had no objective measures of subjective experience and because subjective experience was considered to be hard to trust or deal with. But there is no substitute for a direct approach to human consciousness, an approach that takes subjective experience as data. Part of the solution to this problem is technical: we now possess laboratory and field methods for establishing the parameters of brain correlation with mental experience. Another part of the solution is conceptual: by focusing on the formal aspects of mental states we remove the distractions and intractability of enormous individual differences in mental content. As we see in Chapter 2, most of the important differences between waking and dreaming can be captured by formal analysis. Content analysis can thus be unburdened from the impossible task of explaining the formal differences between states of consciousness.

Chapter 2
Why did the analysis of dream content fail to become a science?

Although there were a few important predecessors of the formal approach to dreaming described in Chapter 1, most dream theorists preferred to focus on content. Impressed with the apparent unintelligibility of dreams, these theorists assumed that there was a rebus, or transformational set of rules (algorithm), which presented the deeper meanings of the dream in disguised symbolic, metaphorical, and sensory terms. Interpretation has always been the main goal of content analysis, whether for medical diagnosis (in the hands of the early Greeks), fortune telling (in the work of Artemidorus), religious prophecy (in the Bible), or psychological divinations (in the proto-scientific schema of Sigmund Freud).

As he was so close to us in time and spirit, and because our brain-based theory is so different from his, in this chapter we focus on Freud's psychoanalytic model as it was developed in his *Project for a Scientific Psychology* (1895) and *The Interpretation of Dreams* (1900). Freud wanted his psychology to have a solid foundation in brain science, but he was 100 years too early to build it as we now can. For this reason, he was forced to resort to speculative philosophy, the medium of all pre-modern dream theories that analyse content. The differences between Freud's content analytical scheme and modern theory are shown in Table 1.

Table 1 Differences between Freud and activation–synthesis:
two models that offer different explanations of the altered state
of dreaming

Dream phenomena	Psychoanalysis	Activation–synthesis
Instigation	Repressed unconscious wish	Brain activation in sleep
Visual imagery	Regression to sensory level	Activation of higher visual centres
Delusional belief	Primary process thinking	Loss of working memory resulting from DLPFC inactivation
Bizarreness	Disguise of wishes	Hyperassociative synthesis
Emotion	Secondary defensive response of ego	Primary activation of limbic system
Forgetting	Repression	Organic (physical) amnesia
Meaning	Actively obscured	Transparent, salient
Interpretation	Needed	Not needed

DLPFC, dorsolateral prefrontal cortex.

For all pre-modern analysts of dream content, the dream as it is
experienced by the dreamer is not what it appears to be; rather,
it is the distorted read-out of a sick body (Greek *Onirodiagnosis*),
or an encoded message about the future from the gods (whether
pagan as with Artemidorus or Judaeo-Christian as in the Bible).
Sigmund Freud picked up the distorted message idea and
acted as the high priest whose psychological skills could tell
the patient things that he would otherwise not know about himself.
All of these systems, including psychoanalysis, are essentially
religions in that they are based on faith in an agency that gives

hidden directives, which can be understood only through the intervention of someone who can interpret the 'message'.

Nourishing these ideas was the general assumption that the world and its people were created by, maintained by, and beholden to a higher power, a god or gods that constituted the ultimate agencies of earthly phenomena. While Freud was an avowed atheist – his rejection of religion was practically phobic – he fell back into the hidden agency idea with his belief in a dynamic unconscious mind that was in constant competition with consciousness. In dreaming, this competition became war-like, so that the mind was forced to resort to extreme defences to avoid being overwhelmed.

At a deeper level, all schemes that analyse content are essentially two-pronged: there are always two agencies – us and them, the body and the spirit, the ego and the id, the brain and the mind. Part of the change in paradigm exemplified by the shift from dream content to dream form is the adoption of the philosophical conviction that the physical world is the only world that there is, that the brain and the mind are therefore inextricably united, and that dreaming is a distinctive form of conscious awareness caused by the state of the brain in sleep. To be fair to Freud, we must acknowledge that he really knew that these things were true (or believed them as fervently as we do), but that the interpretive tradition was too powerful and too tempting for him to resist, especially as he knew next to nothing about the brain.

Still, we can express our astonishment at the failure of so many dream theorists to grasp the dream form theory. When Leonardo da Vinci asked:

'Why does the eye see a thing more clearly in dreams than when awake?'

Can dreams foretell the future?

Since time immemorial, the mysterious nature of dreaming, which we now know is determined mainly by its formal qualities, has led people to believe that dreams were messages from the other world. Dreams have been regarded as prophetic communications which, when properly decoded, would enable us to foretell the future.

There is absolutely no scientific evidence for this theory and considerable scientific evidence against it. It is certainly true that individuals who are concerned about a traumatic event, such as the threat of the loss of a loved one who is sick, will dream about that loved one more than would otherwise be the case. We know from our experiments on lucid dreaming that it is possible to influence dream content simply by having a subject in mind while going to sleep. Therefore, dreaming about a loved one at a time when that loved one's life is threatened is not in the least bit surprising. If the dreamer then calls and finds that the individual has died, it is understandable for him or her to assume that the dream was a premonition of that death. But this is a mistake. It is simply a coincidental correspondence between a situation about which one has legitimate and intense concern and the occurrence of the event that one fears.

We can turn the question around and ask what constitutes scientific proof of the occurrence of dreams that are premonitions (premonitory dreams). The answer is that we would need to do what are called prospective studies, studies in which many individuals are sampled in terms of their

> dream life and judges who know nothing about the dreams or individuals (i.e. are blinded) are asked to make predictions or correspondences between these dream events and events that occurred in real life. A problem that arises here is that individuals who believe in premonitory dreams will usually give one or two striking examples of 'hits', but they never tell you how many premonitory dreams they had that were *not* associated with the event that in fact occurred. To do a scientific study of dream prophecy, we would need to establish some base of how commonly coincidental correspondences occur between dream and waking reality. Until we have that evidence, it is better to believe that the assumption is false.

We would expect such a great genius to offer the speculative but naturalistic answer:

'Because the visual image production system of the brain is selectively activated in sleep!'

And when Shakespeare ascribes to Bottom the recognition that 'I dreamed a dream so strange as to pass all understanding', why doesn't he go on and close the circle by hypothesizing that:

'Because the brain's memory mechanisms are so seriously disrupted during sleep we cannot escape bizarre mental experiences that would otherwise occur only during madness.'

Indeed, the analogy with madness offers clues about the creation of dreams by the brain precisely because the form of dreaming is very much like certain kinds of madness. The combination of frequent visual hallucinations (in the perceptual domain), instability of orientation, and recent memory loss (in the cognitive domain) should have made physicians, such as Sigmund Freud and Carl Jung, recognize that the mental illness that dreaming simulated best was delirium, the psychosis associated with the acute brain dysfunctions caused by toxicity (alcohol and drugs), anoxia (inadequate supply of oxygen to the brain caused by circulation deficiencies), and acute head trauma. Jung said, 'Let the dreamer awake and you will see psychosis.' Fair enough. But what kind of psychosis will you see? The fact that it is delirium should have suggested that a major shift in brain function was necessary to account for such a major change in mental state. We return to this discussion in Chapter 7.

With regard to mental state, we need to note two important points: one phenomenological, the other methodological.

For phenomenology, the term 'mental state' implies global features: every aspect of mental activity changes when the mental state changes. The easiest way to effect a global change in mental state is to engineer a global change in brain state. For methodology, the clinical assessment of mental state has always been achieved by an examination known as the mental status exam. Uniting neurology and psychiatry, the mental status exam is a comprehensive checklist of mind functions that are known to be disrupted by organic brain disease, i.e. brain disease caused by a physical rather than a mental condition.

To introduce the far-reaching implications of dream science to a general science of consciousness, consider the following categories of the mental status exam:

- Consciousness: clear or clouded?
- Attention: focused or distractible?
- Intellectual: sharp functions or dull?
- Perceptions: externally driven or hallucinated?
- Cognition: logical or illogical?

- Emotion: stable or unstable/uncontrolled?
- Memory: good or poor?
- Abstraction: symbolic or concrete?

Even this very incomplete list makes us realize how careless we have been in not applying the mental state concept to dreaming and the mental status approach to its analysis.

Below is another report that will help us see the global nature of mental state changes in dreaming:

9/3/1981 Red Car, Dream no. 16

I am trying to organize a group for a departure. I find one member at the foot of a hill, near some water. I urge him to go up the hill to a rendezvous point for departure.

Suddenly, or perhaps always, he is in a red car, which runs along beside me up the hill. The peculiar thing is that the front of the car, including the driver, is underground. Yet its trajectory is smooth and the ground is unbroken!

As we climb, the car moves ahead of me and I make a strong but vain effort to keep up with its progress. The car then crosses from

left to right and runs – still half underground – into a wall. I wonder if the driver will have hurt his head in the crash.

  The scene changes.

  I am in a locker room and approach my son Ian who has been hurt. At first his legs appear to have been amputated at the knees and I feel dread. But as I approach, what I took to be stumps are his blood-smeared kneecaps (very bright red blood – like the car – and he is smiling, not crying). I am relieved and wake up.

My *consciousness* is clear as a bell. In fact, I see – and feel –everything in this dream with a *surreal intensity* that would have pleased André Breton as much as Leonardo da Vinci. The intense hallucinatory *percepts* grip my *attention* in a vice that won't let it do anything else but watch in fascination – and in *horror* – as the half-buried car hurtles uphill and crashes despite my effort to control it. The emotions of *horror* and *dread* (*fear*) survive the scene shift – to the locker room – where I am *relieved* to find that my son is OK. Although it is not explicitly noted, my cognition is defective and my logical reasoning poor. How could the car do what it appeared to do and without disrupting the ground? 'Seeing is believing' is one answer.

My Red Car dream reveals another kind of association – one marked by a high degree of emotional salience. My son, Ian, *was* badly injured in an automobile accident and one of his legs *was* threatened and saved. So it is natural for my memory of associations – associative memory – to link the red car crash to my son, Ian. *But* (and it is a large *but*) I do not see Ian in the hospital setting where I actually beheld him at the time of his accident. And he had only one leg damaged, not two. This departure of the dream scenario from long-term memory of personal experiences, called episodic memory in psychological terminology, is typical and needs to be explained. Episodic memory may feed dream content useful fragments for plot construction, but it does not supply the details that are, in waking, so easily remembered. Why? What is going on? We should not ignore cases like this because there is nothing less at stake than how memory works. This means that dream science is a set of rules for understanding unconscious aspects of memory formation, but not in the sense intended by theorists who analyse dream content.

Extending the suggestions of Chapter 1, dream science now needs much more careful consideration of the numerous subcategories of mental state. A list of such subcategories and the ways that neurobiology explains them are given in Table 2. Having stumbled, almost by accident, on the now obvious fact that the bizarreness of dreams is a reflection of orientational instability, we want to know much more about other memory functions. Are declarative and/or episodic memories used in dream plot constructions? To what extent and with what constraints? The terms 'declarative' and 'episodic' refer to specific memories of personal or historical events, e.g. I went to Boston last weekend. This kind of memory is contrasted with 'semantic' memory, which consists of general facts, e.g. Boston is the capital of Massachusetts. Another class of memory is 'procedural', e.g. I know how to drive my car to Boston.

And what about thinking? We already know that thinking is suppressed in dreaming and that it is only slightly effective when it does appear.

Among the generally unsung heroes of the dream form theory, brain state = mental state, looms the Romantic Movement figure of David Hartley, who lived at the turn of the 19th century, famous as the father of British Associationism. Associationism asserts that memory is organized according to categorical similarities among objects, people, ideas, and so on, to every category of content. A good example, from my Richard Newland dream in Chapter 1, is the associative linking of spray painting with sulphating of grapevines. Although the purposes are very different, the processes are similar – to cover a large surface area with liquid, it is useful to turn the liquid into tiny particles and to spread these via a pressurized vapour system. Another example, in the Red Car

dream, is the association of the hallucinated car crash with my
son's accident.

Table 2 The physiological basis for the differences between waking and
sleeping consciousness. The causal hypotheses listed in column three
are explained later in this book

Function	Nature of difference	Hypothesis of cause
Sensory input	Blocked	Presynaptic inhibition
Perception (external)	Diminished	Blockade of sensory input
Perception (internal)	Enhanced	Disinhibition of networks storing sensory representations
Attention	Lost	Decreased aminergic modulation
Memory (recent)	Diminished	Because of aminergic demodulation, activated representations are not restored in memory
Memory (remote)	Enhanced	Disinhibition of networks storing mnemonic representations increases access to consciousness
Orientation	Unstable	Internally inconsistent orienting signals are generated by cholinergic system
Thought	Reasoning ad hoc Logical rigour weak Processing hyperassociative	Loss of attention, memory, and volition leads to failure of sequencing and rule inconstancy; analogy replaces analysis

Insight	Self-reflection lost	Failures of attention, logic, and memory weaken second- (and third-) order representations
Language (internal)	Confabulatory	Aminergic demodulation frees narrative synthesis from logical restraints
Emotion	Episodically strong	Cholinergic hyperstimulation of amygdala and related temporal lobe structures in the brain triggers emotional storms which are unmodulated by aminergic restraint
Instinct	Episodically strong	Cholinergic hyperstimulation of hypothalamus and limbic forebrain triggers fixed action motor programmes, which are experienced fictitiously but not enacted
Volition	Weak	Top-down motor control and frontal executive power cannot compete with disinhibited subcortical network activation
Output	Blocked	Postsynaptic inhibition

From J. Allan Hobson and Edward Pace-Schott, *Fundamental Neuroscience*, 2nd edn., Nov. 2002

What caused the failure of psychoanalytic dream theory?

Freud must have had in mind the fragmentary nature involved in incorporating episodic memory when he coined the term 'day residue' and dubbed it the dream stimulus. Subsequent scientific work on memory sources of dreams has shown, however, that even this notion is mistaken. In Tore Nielsen's data, the incorporation of confidently identified memory sources is actually low for the day immediately preceding a given night's dream; it becomes higher as one moves backwards in time to a peak at day 6 before dreaming. In the French neurophysiologist Michel Jouvet's dream data, the peak of incorporation is 7 days before the dream and never includes content from locales to which he has just travelled, a surprise even for theories that emphasize emotional salience, as well as those that emphasize recency.

Freud's work suffered from two fatal scientific defects, which his brilliant rhetoric could not overcome. One was the absence of relevant brain science, which he knew was indispensable and would some day force revision of his theories. For this he cannot be blamed. He was a creature of his time and his ambition pushed him a century ahead of that time. But because Freud *was* trained as a biological scientist, we can in all fairness ask why he was so careless as an observer. Why were his data so limited? Why was his focus so narrowly fixed?

As far as the data are concerned, Freud made no attempt to collect dream reports from people other than himself, and even those reports are few in number (about 40 are cited in the 700 pages of his *Interpretation of Dreams*) and fragmentary (his word counts, of less than 100, are many times less than most modern samples). In the 1890s, as today, it was an easy matter to collect an extensive, representative sample and to treat the data-set as a whole rather than using the piecemeal, axe-grinding, controversial technique that Freud used to discuss each one.

Freud's scholarship is evident in his detailed discussion of the scientific literature before 1900. However, he is controversial and exclusive rather than dispassionate and balanced in discussing the work of others. In many cases, his derisive dismissals seem justified, but, for one who was sure that the brain was important, he is cavalier in his treatment of such intellectual giants as Wilhelm Wundt (who correctly assumed that the dreaming brain would show a selective increase in some of its functions, e.g. vision, and a selective decrease in others, e.g. memory and reasoning). For Freud, the idea that any dream content was nonsensical, i.e. gratuitously associative, was anathema. He therefore thought that Wundt's suggestion that the bizarre nature of dreams reflects a delirious series of links of loosely connected contents must be wrong.

Freud ignored two important predecessors. One was David Hartley, who ascribed the bizarre nature of dreams to too many associations; he had a functional theory to go with his hypothesis, a hypothesis that was probably correct. Dreaming, for Hartley, served to loosen associations that were otherwise inclined to become obsessively fixed. 'And that would be madness,' Hartley asserted. Certainly, dreaming is a hyperassociative state (i.e. a state in which many, many associations are made), as Freud could have quickly determined had he examined dream reports before rushing to interpret them.

The second great predecessor was Wundt's teacher, Herman Helmholtz, who also inspired Freud's own mentor, Herman Muller, and helped to create the anti-vitalist spirit of the age in which Freud's theory took root. In discussing dreaming in his classic *Physiological Optics*, Helmholtz was a formalist in his approach to hallucinated movement. As Helmholtz noticed, the sense of the self moving through the dream space is one of the most robust formal features of dreaming. When today we refer to 'sensorimotor hallucinations' we are only echoing Helmholtz's recognition that the dreaming brain is capable of simulating acts of movement (motor acts) extremely convincingly. Helmholtz recognized that this meant that motor control – in waking – must be highly predictive. More specifically he theorized that the nervous system created its own image of the expected consequence of movement.

This principle has become enshrined in movement physiology as the 'efferent copy hypothesis'. If, and only if, we are able to predict, and project, an image of movement outcomes are we able to move effectively. The almost magical ease of dream movement (witness my weightless gliding and the flight patterns of lucid dreamers) is due to this self-contained, closed-loop activation, in sleep, of movement patterns that are felt by us to be complete and have an outcome. This, of course, implies activation of generators of motor patterns in the brain, for which there is now abundant evidence.

The best that poor old Freud could do with flying dreams was to argue that they represented displaced sexual desire. Freud's rebus, you will recall, was that unconscious wishes – and sexual wishes needed to be kept unconscious – escaped the censor's denunciation when the ego was weakened by sleep. If the now free-to-be-expressed sexual impulses were not disguised, by the pleasurable but not sexual hallucination of flying, the dreamer would be awakened by the consciousness of these forbidden desires. Freud never mentioned his own sexual dreams. Perhaps he never had any – or never remembered them. But this is unlikely. And any research participant – or any of his patients – could have told him that sexual dreams, complete with orgasm, occur in the very same people who enjoy flying dreams.

The kind of argument that I am now advancing is dismissed as Freud-bashing by the many, still passionate defenders of psychoanalysis. It is true that I want to discredit Freud emphatically, but only because we are all still in danger of accepting subsequent psychological explanations for dream phenomena that are likely to have physiological mechanisms with quite different psychological meanings from those that we can now imagine. For example, we might experience exotic movement, including sexual movement, in dreams in order to refresh movement programmes that are crucial to survival. We might also regard dreams as efforts to revise those programmes in terms of emotionally salient or important memories. Thus, my son's accident is an important aspect of my bicycle dream. In fact, he had another terrible accident on a bicycle before we stopped him from riding with his own impaired motor control system. Ian's bike accident is fixed in my memory as a warning: this could happen again to him and to me.

Can associations ever really be free?

Associations are not associations unless they have meaningful connections. The meaning of their connection is determined as much by the context in which they are evoked as by their historical source. So, just as Freud, the atheist, was doomed by his authoritarian speculations to create a new religion of which he was the highest of priests, so he was destined to suggest certain associations for the dream content of his clients, even as he tried desperately to distance himself from hypnosis and the criticism of suggestibility. This was particularly true of his work with hysterical patients, whose highly hypnotizable nature he recognized. And he knew from his experience at the Salpêtrière Hospital in Paris in 1885, that the neurologists Pierre Janet and Jean-Martin Charcot were able to get whatever result they wanted from their hysterical patients, especially in the theatrical context of medical teaching amphitheatres.

Freud's idea that he could avoid suggesting content by laying a client down on a couch (encouraging a pre-sleep relaxation) and sitting behind him or her (to remove any personal impact) seems grossly naïve in retrospect. Sleep onset is a particularly fruitful state for the elaboration of fantasy and dream-like mental activity that incorporated local conditions shamelessly. And any patient, hysterical or not, would know – by 1910 at the very latest – what Freud expected in the way of 'associations'. Now that the false memory phenomenon is so well known, it is easy for us to see what mischief Freud's 'scientific' precautions must have cost him. To avoid repeating these mistakes, we need to be much more critical, and much more versatile, than Freud was.

One way to free the formal approach to dreaming for immunity from the charge of self-fulfilling prophecy is to keep our mind genuinely open with respect to psychological meaning, to resist any formulaic approach to interpretation, and to refuse any interpretation that is not straightforward and tied to physiology. This means that we have to settle for less than Freud wanted. As made clear in Chapter 11, there remain many aspects of dreaming that we cannot explain today, although, as this book attempts to show, many aspects of dream content *can* be explained today using the formal approach. Those that cannot be explained will have to wait. But, with the field moving as fast as it is today, the wait will not be long, and it will be worthwhile because we will finally obtain what Freud could only dream of: a psychology that is perspicacious and free from doubt.

Brain–mind isomorphism and the science of dreaming

The word 'isomorphism' means similarity of form or shape, and brain–mind isomorphism that every form of mental activity has a similar form of brain activity. Therefore, if we detect a dream form, we can seek a corresponding brain form. In dreaming, the simplest example is activation. To explain the awakening of the mind in sleep we should expect to find a similar (but not of course identical) awakening of the brain during sleep. As we see in Chapter 3, we do find this – the brain is electrically activated in sleep and, when this happens, the mind is turned on too. Naturally. It's that simple.

A more detailed example should clinch our point. If, in our exploration of the brain in sleep, we find physiological evidence that memory systems are disabled, we should expect to find that memory is altered during dreaming and that dreams would be difficult to recall. We already know that the second prediction is true, but just how true we cannot yet say precisely. The first prediction has, however, scarcely been entertained. Is it generally true that I cannot exercise my episodic memory when I am dreaming? Does this affect dream content?

These examples are chosen to highlight two important points about the doctrine of brain–mind isomorphism. One is that it is just as fruitful to map from the brain to the mind as it is to map from the mind to the brain. The second is that we must choose carefully the appropriate level of each domain at which to focus our isomorphic efforts. In the beginning, and we are still very much at the beginning, we will find that global and psychologically general levels will be more generous than detailed and psychologically personal ones. Individual differences have never been generous to psychology. And how many of them are real? Although it may disappoint you if you hanker after a fortune-telling interpretation of your dreams, our attention to the mirrored formal aspects is necessary to the scientific understanding of dreaming as a universal process. Later in this book we will see how it can be used to help individual dream interpretation by relieving it of an impossibly difficult task and helping us to discover the usually clear emotional salience of our dreams.

Chapter 3
How is the brain activated in sleep?

Consciousness is so rapidly and dramatically reduced during sleep that it was natural to assume that the brain simply turned off at sleep onset and turned on again just before awakening. Indeed, some people do sleep all night in that deep, oblivious, and uninterrupted way. Some, but by no means all. And no one sleeps that way all the time. There are periods of life change and stress when mental activity seems to go on all night. Are these to be attributed to our not really being able to sleep at such times? Perhaps. But what about dreaming? How could such elaborate and exciting mental activity arise in an inactive brain?

This question was answered in a wide variety of erroneous ways. As dream recall was generally poor and needed awakening to be present at all, many scientists – Sigmund Freud among them – wrongly assumed that dreaming occurred only in the instant before awakening. Now it is certainly true that dreaming can occur just before awakening. And we have already noted that dreaming can be so unpleasantly exciting as to provoke awakening, leading to another erroneous assumption: that all dreams are unpleasantly exciting, i.e. all dreams are characterized by negative emotions such as anger, anxiety, or fear.

Another erroneous theory was that dreaming arose in response to external sensory stimuli that were strong enough to activate the brain, but not strong enough to produce arousal. Again it is true that train whistles, indigestion, and spouses coming home late can influence dream content. But they often don't, and dreaming doesn't depend on such stimuli even when they do gain entry to the sleeping brain.

It turns out that most dreaming occurs under the calm cover of sleep and is the result of a built-in mechanism of brain activation that operates in all of us every night of our lives. It is the goal of this chapter to explain how the brain activation of sleep was discovered and how it gradually initiated the paradigm shift, or change in strategy, from dream content to dream form that has been the subject of my first two chapters. Before beginning our story, it is important to appreciate that, just as it took a full half-century (1900–53) to recognize the reality of brain activation in sleep, it has taken another half-century (1953–2003) for us to come to terms with this discovery. And there are still many die-hards who refuse to relinquish the hopeless fantasy of the total power of interpretation offered by dream content analysis.

Why did it take so long to discover brain activation in sleep?

We are inclined to assume that it is the slow progress of technological development that impeded scientific advances in studying dreaming. But this is a face-saving sop for those who were so conceptually blinded that they could not imagine the simple experiments that could have led to the brain activation conclusion. As Michel Jouvet shows in his novel *Château du Rêve*, most of our vaunted twentieth-century discoveries about sleep could have been made earlier by the most useful scientific instrument of all: direct observation. The direct observability of sleep is especially easy to achieve in our infants and children, the very individuals who most dramatically reveal the brain activation of rapid eye movement (REM) in their behaviour.

And it almost happened, although never quite. Instead of simply observing sleepers – and seeing with one's own eyes the periodic occurrence of small facial and eye movements, as well as muffled cries, penile erection, flaccid muscle tone, depressed spinal reflexes, and a host of other autonomic or self-regulating measures (take respiratory rate for a simple example) – those few scientists who were interested enough to perform anything faintly resembling a sleep or dream experiment interfered with the sleep of the participants in their studies. It was the induction of dreaming that these scholars, most of whom were French, were interested in. Could they induce a participant to dream of a certain odour by opening a perfume bottle under his or her nose? The answer was yes, as they found out, but it was very, very difficult. And, meanwhile, they missed the chance to observe natural sleep.

We must admit that staying up all night observing other people sleeping is not everyone's idea of fun. It requires unusual motivation and a modicum of self-discipline, even if one is tempted by the prospect of discovery. If Freud had only imagined that dream behaviour could be observed – he was certainly motivated enough to do it – he would quickly have realized that all he needed to do to be a sharp observer was to sleep in the daytime. His phobic concern about suggestion could have been further quieted by the premium placed upon doing nothing but watching.

But, in reality, it's even easier than that. For anyone to observe REM sleep behaviour directly, it can be done with bed partners, especially in the wee hours of the morning, most conveniently on vacation, in the summer time when the hillock of the cornea can be seen in the early dawn light to glide to and fro under the closed – or perhaps half-open – eyelids. The eyelids themselves dance and twitch sporadically and, when they do, one has only to give a light tap on the shoulder and ask what is going on in the mind. Informed consent is as admirable in these informal conditions as it is in university sleep labs, but don't let that stop you.

If you don't have a willing bed partner, you can observe your big sister's baby or anyone's pet cat or dog, and have the same thrill of discovery. Of course you can't expect an answer if you ask *them* if they are dreaming. But you can answer that question for yourself now that you know that the REMs that give brain-activated sleep its most popular name are a direct readout of the internal activation. Not that dreaming occurs exclusively in REM sleep. It doesn't. REM sleep just happens to provide the most ideal condition for its occurrence.

In Chapter 4, we take up the question about the dreaming brain that, so far, only our animal collaborators can answer; in Chapter 5, we consider the implication for the development of the abundant, florid REM sleep of all mammalian newborns. My point here is simple and descriptive. The first step of any natural history endeavour is to observe (quietly and carefully) and to record one's observations (thoroughly and systematically). It is as embarrassing as it is instructive that this was never done by anyone aspiring to either sleep or dream science before 1930. How many other breakthrough discoveries now elude us because we are conceptually boxed in by gratuitous assumptions that there is nothing to observe and/or that we can obviate direct observation via intuition or speculation?

The electroencephalogram and the sleep lab

Neurophysiologists were every bit as slow as psychologists to move dream science forwards. They knew about reflexes but they didn't know about spontaneous activation. Instead they assumed that the brain was as dependent on stimulation for all of its activated states as was the mind in sleep.

Two of the greatest minds in the history of science studied reflexes and believed that mental activity was stimulus-dependent. The Nobel Laureate Charles Sherrington argued, forcefully, that the reflex was the functional unit of the brain. He never really listened to his imaginative student, Thomas Graham Brown, who tried to convince Sherrington that it was the spontaneous activity of paired 'half-centres' that set the stage for reflex responsiveness. The basic difference between Sherrington's reflex and Graham Brown's half-centre concept is that the reflex brain was completely dependent upon external stimuli, unlike the half-centre brain which was capable of spontaneous activity. Sherrington made the mistake of assuming from his own conscious experience that his brain simply turned off when he went to sleep.

Ivan Pavlov, justifiably famous for showing that reflexes can be conditioned, shared Sherrington's assumption that the mind was blank in sleep (wrong!) because the brain was inactive (wrong again!) and unstimulated (wrong once again!). As we see in Chapter 4, it was not until well after the discovery of REM sleep that the activation of the nerve elements known as neurons (neuronal activation) was shown to be continuous in sleep. This means that our brains never turn off completely, and hence they are always capable of *some* level of mental activity, even if waking and dream consciousness both depend on a robust level of brain activation.

Electrophysiology began to correct the picture in 1928 when the German psychiatrist Adolf Berger succeeded in recording brain waves from the surface of his patients' heads using an amplification and recording device that came to be known as the electroencephalograph (or EEG). The EEG revolutionized sleep and dream science as much as it altered clinical neurology because it provided an objective tool for assessing dynamic brain activity in normal individuals as well as in patients with epilepsy. Figure 2 illustrates an EEG, together with other variables used in modern sleep science. Against great scepticism that his so-called 'brain waves' were artefacts of movement or muscle activity, Berger won the day when he showed that the EEG underwent distinctive changes in sleep. To cut a long story short, behavioural sleep was invariably associated with a tendency for the brain waves to slow (in frequency) and to increase (in amplitude). This change marks

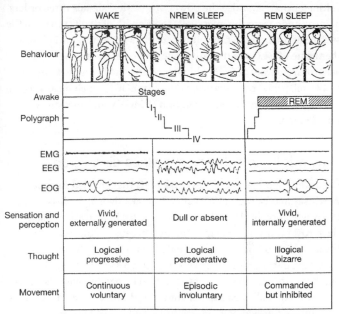

	WAKE	NREM SLEEP	REM SLEEP
Behaviour			
Polygraph	Awake — Stages I, II, III, IV		REM
EMG			
EEG			
EOG			
Sensation and perception	Vivid, externally generated	Dull or absent	Vivid, internally generated
Thought	Logical progressive	Logical perseverative	Illogical bizarre
Movement	Continuous voluntary	Episodic involuntary	Commanded but inhibited

2. **Behavioural states in humans.** States of waking, NREM sleep, and REM sleep have behavioural, polygraphic, and psychological manifestations. The sequence of these stages is represented in the polygraph channel. Sample tracings of three variables used to distinguish state are also shown: electromyogram (EMG), which is highest in waking, intermediate in NREM sleep, and lowest in REM sleep; the electroencephalogram (EEG) and electro-oculogram (EOG), which are both activated in waking and REM sleep and inactivated in NREM sleep. Each sample is approximately 20 seconds.

the onset of what we now call slow wave or non-REM (NREM) sleep.

It wasn't long before the EEG was used to study sleep in the forerunners of today's sleep labs. The capacity to record physiological variables has grown so dramatically in the twentieth century that we tend to forget how simple the early devices were, and how startling the discoveries made with them. Today's 'polygraphs' are all direct descendants of Berger's baby, a glorified voltmeter that can raise the power of electrical signals three orders of magnitude from the microvolt (thousandth of a volt) range on the surface of the body to the volt range of the recorders. Variations on the theme of EEG are its better-known predecessors, the electrocardiogram (ECG), which measures the heart's activity, and its two offspring, the electro-oculogram (EOG), which measures eye movement, and the electromyogram (EMG), which measures muscle tone.

How was brain activation in sleep discovered?

It was the combination of EEG and EOG that enabled Eugene Aserinsky and Nathaniel Kleitman to make their 1953 discovery of brain activation in sleep. They called the brain activation phase of sleep REM (for rapid eye movements) because of the association of the activation of the eye movements (oculomotor activation) with activation of the brain. They asserted that dreaming might be another associated event. It was the EMG (together with the EEG and EOG) that allowed Michel Jouvet and François Michel to show that muscle tone supporting posture – and hence postural movement – was actively abolished in REM sleep.

Before 1953, it was recognized that sleep was not uniform/intractable, any more than it was inert. In other words, electrical patterns of brain-wave activity changed continuously, denoting both global and local flows of brain activation. It was assumed, erroneously, that only the intense brain activation of REM was capable of sustaining dreaming. As the REM periods occurred periodically at 90-minute intervals and occupied 1.5 to 2 hours per night, this seemed like more than enough time to accommodate dreaming. It is certainly many times more than the instant before awakening.

It turns out, however, that dreaming can also occur at sleep onset (no surprise because the EEG is still relatively activated) and in other phases of so-called NREM sleep, especially late night stage II

> ## Do we dream in black and white or in colour?
>
> Modern lab evidence suggests strongly that we dream in colour. To what, then, do we attribute the common misperception that dreaming occurs in black and white? The answer is very clear – it is the poor memory. Recall of dreaming is a function not only of brain activation in sleep but also of awakening conditions, which determine whether dreams will be recalled at all, whether they will be recalled clearly, and whether they will be recalled at length. In all clear, lengthy reports we see colour descriptors in abundance. We dream in colour. In our thousands of lab dream reports, there is not a single instance of a well-recalled dream being in black and white, as would be expected if this were indeed normally the case.

sleep when the brain is almost as active as in REM sleep, often called stage I. That leaves stages III and IV, which occur early in the night and are considerably less likely to be associated with dreaming.

The point of this introduction to sleep lab science is to show that, although technology was not really necessary to describe dreaming scientifically or to describe sleep behaviourally (because both could have been done via careful direct observation), it was indispensable in showing that brain activity is continuous – and continuously variable – in sleep.

Who discovered REM and the EEG sleep cycle?

Eugene Aserinsky was interested in studying attention in children, so sleep was a nuisance to him because, no matter how hard he tried to keep them alert, sleep invariably took over the minds of his young participants. As many teachers of the young have seen, Aserinsky noticed that when his participants' attention flagged their eyes tended to close. He therefore decided to put electrodes near the childrens' eyes in order to record their eye movements while they were awake, and this helped. Aserinsky was, however, astonished to discover that, when his young participants finally succumbed to sleep, their eyes darted back and forth and up and down behind their closed lids. He had inadvertently discovered REM sleep – and the first participant was his seven-year-old son Armand. Aserinsky was a persistent scientist but he was also just plain lucky. Why? Because REM occurs at sleep onset *only* in children!

As Louis Pasteur opined, 'In the field of observation chance favours the prepared mind'. When Aserinsky reported his observations to Kleitman, his mentor recognized their significance for a science of dreaming. By extending this observation on the eyes into sleep, and by recording the EEG and the heart and respiratory rates in adults, Aserinsky and Kleitman were able to observe the regular ebb and flow of activation affecting the brain, the eyes, the heart, and even breathing throughout sleep. When this activation was maximal – with a wake-like EEG, clusters of REMs, rapid heart action, and fast, shallow breathing – awakenings yielded long, complex dream reports, similar to the one below.

11/7/1981 Country House in Winter, Dream no. 19

We are at a country house in winter, like the farm in East Burke but different. K.D.K. is there and we are skiing. I am looking, with a sexual motive, for A.T. whom I have not seen for at least 20 years and whom I never loved. She may be upstairs in this home, which may or may not be mine. The second floor is reached by climbing a twisted wooden shaft with inadequate branch-like steps. It is a struggle. When I pull myself up – noting that the heating is on and therefore that the house must be inhabited – I find myself in the arms of a sleeping J.C.

J.C. suddenly wakes up – with a look of not-surprising terror on

his face – and tries to orient himself. I see and feel his murderous, self-protective fear as he struggles to decide if I am I, and if I am real. This all happens in an intense instant, summarizing all of the emotional complexity of our relationship. I try to reassure him saying, 'J.C., it's me, I love you.' And. . . .

Dreams with frankly sexual themes such as this one are relatively rare in sleep lab settings, where being the content is more likely to reflect concern about sleeping while being observed and being subjected to awakening. (In fact, this dream occurred when I was on a trip to China and sleeping in a hotel in Guangzhou, of which there is not the faintest record in my dream.) The dream is, however, typical of those reported after awakenings from REM sleep, whether in the sleep lab using the Aserinsky–Kleitman theory, at home using our portable Nightcap monitoring system, or in hotels in Guangzhou, China.

11/7/1981 Country House in Winter, Dream no. 20

I am again climbing toward an ambiguous bedroom. This time the thread of the spiral ascent is to the left upward. There are two routes: one is safe, but long, through grass at the base of a rock butte; I take the other, more vertical and direct ascent on the edge of

the rocks. I am glad that I was forewarned (by C.?) that the rock was rotten because I quickly adapt to the succession of slides of large slabs of the cliff side. Each time I take a step, some of the granite falls away. These huge chunks of rock make not a sound as they fall, out of view, to my left. Finally, with relief, I am at the summit, which is a grill-like threshold on to which I level myself with two hands. I thank my benefactress – hostess (C.?) for having prepared me to cope with this hazardous ascent.

The universal characteristics that this REM sleep dream evinces are intense frequent hallucinations (called hallucinosis in psychology) – in this case the climbing movements are all perilously gripping – and a complete lack of self-reflective awareness. The setting is typically indefinite: it is my house but not really; the characters are vaguely defined – in this case particularly C.; emotions such as fear and elation are strong.

It is as if my brain were activated in a particular, selective way to form hallucinations and emotions that are sensorimotor (coordinating perception and action) in character, causing these elements to be combined in a completely novel but personally meaningful way. This is the 'synthesis' part of the dream process that Robert McCarley and I wanted to identify in our 1977 activation–synthesis thesis. In Chapter 5, we learn more about evidence for this hypothesis, which can come through the application of imaging techniques to sleep and dream science.

During the early days of the sleep lab era (about 1953–75), the goal was to establish correlations between details of the dream plot, as described by participants, and details of physiology, as described by the EEG or polygraph. I call this the strong one-to-one isomorphic hypothesis, which attempts to link mental activity to peripheral physiology in real time. The goal was not achieved. Thus, early claims that the eye movements of REM sleep could be predicted from the sequence of directional changes in the dreamer's hallucinated gaze could not be substantiated. Although dream content did occasionally reflect the sudden increases and decreases of respiratory efforts, as would be expected in turning, talking, or painting, more often it did not.

In retrospect, the failure of this ambitious theory is not surprising: it never worked very well in waking either. It perpetuates the notion of the philosopher and psychologist William James, who held that emotion was the perception of peripheral physiology (e.g. anxiety occurs when I sense my rapid heart rate). This idea was discredited and eclipsed by Walter Cannon and Philip Bard's centralist theory of emotion, which says that the feelings that we have are a function of selective activation of that part of the brain known as the limbic brain (see Figure 11); they may then be associated with a wide variety of peripheral physiological changes.

An even more serious disconnection between dream psychology and brain physiology was threatened. When first David Foulkes, and later many other psychologists, reported that dreaming *could* be associated with almost any EEG stage of sleep, they reached the unlikely conclusion that the mental activity of dreams had nothing to do with sleep neurophysiology. Believe it or not, this mind–brain dissociation hypothesis is still passionately defended. Needless to say, most of those who held these views were the disappointed champions of strong content analysis; some were even die-hard Freudians, and none was a practitioner of physiological sleep science.

Among the many compelling reasons to reject the assertion of brain–mind dissociation is the still overwhelming evidence that REM sleep is the most favourable base for fully realized and sustained dreaming; that NREM sleep is at best only half as favourable; that sleep onset is even less so; and that while awake, dreaming is essentially impossible. At this stage of our scientific knowledge all we can say is that dreaming is increasingly probable if the several brain conditions of REM sleep are present. The psychological counterpart of this correlation is given by the formal analysis and not content analysis of dreams. In dream reports we therefore seek to measure the degree to which they are hallucinatory (not what is seen) or thoughtful (not what is thought).

What is the biology of sleep and dream science?

Meanwhile, even as the dream debate grew fractious and became sterile, the sleep lab was unearthing a treasure trove of physiological findings of great interest to dream science, as well as to behavioural biology generally. The Aserinsky–Kleitman discovery was made in 1953, the same year that Watson and Crick published their epochal double-helix model for DNA. There are two important implications of this coincidence. One is that biology came of molecular age at the same moment that dream science came of physiological age. In the subsequent half-century, biology has changed beyond recognition – in fact, it is now in danger of becoming nothing but the molecular biology of the gene.

Sleep and dream science, meanwhile, has only begun to approach molecular biology in terms of either conceptual ideas or methodology. This is both because the descriptive task of sleep and dream science was so enormous and because the concepts that were drawn into the field, especially from psychology, were not equal to the scientific opportunities presented. Not everyone, even today, wants to make mental activity physical. Too many cultural and private belief systems are threatened by the idea that consciousness in dreaming, as in waking, is a brain function. The immortality of the soul is a prime example. If the brain dies, doesn't the mind die with it?

One idea that the biological revolution in dream science forces us to take seriously is that, although it constitutes an undeniably interesting and informative state of altered consciousness, dreaming has no particular function in and of itself. As conscious experience, dreaming is nothing but our occasional awareness of brain activation in sleep. In this view, it is the brain activation underlying REM sleep itself that performs the vaunted functions of dreaming: establishing psychic equilibrium, integrating recent and past learning, casting our inventory of personal information in emotionally salient (or relevant) terms. All of these important functions can and certainly must be performed whether or not we are aware of them. If they depended on our conscious awareness of dreaming, we would be in big trouble – especially those who have no dream recall whatsoever.

The burden of proof now falls clearly, and heavily, on those who maintain that an awareness of dream content actually helps us. For example, I am enlightened by finding through recall of Dream no. 19 that my psychosexual conflicts with a former friend and his wife are still alive in my mind. But, even if my interpretation of this dream is correct, how does it help me to know this fact? By making me aware that yes, after all, there is an unconscious, or that yes, after all, sexuality *is* polymorphous and ambiguous – that despite superficial appearances to the contrary, all is not entirely kosher in Hobson's unconscious mind.

Such sophistication might endear me to my psychoanalytic

brethren, leading to a wider acceptance of my ideas, increased book royalties, and even referral of patients. Thus, my physical survival as well as my intellectual procreation could be enhanced. But it seems far more likely that I would do as well, or better, if I never had my spiral staircase dream or, rather, never recalled and therefore never interpreted it – the 'dream work', if any, is done unbeknownst to me, by REM sleep and its friends in my unconscious brain.

This is just the kind of 'reductionism' that psychologist opponents of physiologically based dream theory fear. Foulkes has argued passionately against what he perceives to be 'physiology's effort to take the problem of dreaming off of psychology's hands'. To some extent he is correct. If the main formal features of dreaming can be shown to be physiologically determined, then content analysis does not have to account for them. Instead of lamenting this situation, however, dream psychology could do well to breathe a heavy sigh of relief at seeing this onerous burden lifted. Freud himself was pushed to the psychoanalytic wall in trying to explain dream hallucinosis as a psychological defence. His effort to explain poor dream memory in terms of active repression (rather than simple amnesia) was equally forced. Worst of all, his effort to account for dream emotion in terms of either wish fulfilment or disguise fell flat on its face because so many dreams contain unpleasant negative affect and because so many are undisguised.

Reductionism was Freud's strong suit. He tried to explain, as all would-be scientists do, the greatest number of variables in terms of the fewest assumptions. In hitting upon his wish fulfilment–disguise censorship model he was reductionist in the extreme. *Every* steeple is a phallus. *Every* dimple is a vagina. The problem is that Freud's reductionism was wrong, and it was wrong, in large part, because he did not observe behaviour, measure neurological function, or collect dreams systematically using the mind-set and tools of natural science.

Now, we have the facts of human sleep physiology. Now, we know –

beyond the shadow of a doubt – that our consciousness in waking, sleeping, or dreaming is a brain function. It is high time to move on and to create the great, bold, and neurobiologically based theory to which Freud himself aspired. Reductionism cannot explain away phenomena. Dreaming will always be vivid, bizarre, emotional, unreasonable, and hard to remember. But how (the question of mechanism) and why (the question of function) may be explored scientifically using physiological tools. As content analytical dream theory reveals, it is the danger of circularity that has given subjectivity a bad name. Now we have a brave new world of scientific dream theory in which circularity can be transcended and dreaming can still be enjoyed, discussed, and interpreted.

In this chapter, we take seriously the idea that it is REM sleep that constitutes the ideal physiological conditions for dreaming, and attempt to use the data collected in cellular and molecular level studies of sleep in animals to answer the how and why questions of dreaming in greater detail.

Chapter 4
Cells and molecules of the dreaming brain

By 1890, the scientific world was aware that the brain consisted of billions of individual cells called neurons (100 billion at the last count). In the first half of the twentieth century, while sleep and dream science were being prepared at the more global level of the electroencephalograph (EEG), neurobiologists were learning more about neurons than had even been imagined in anyone's speculative philosophy – and that anyone includes Sigmund Freud, Charles Sherrington, and Ivan Pavlov.

Among other things, by 1950 it had become clear that, as each neuron was bounded by a semipermeable membrane, it had the capacity to concentrate an electrical charge across that membrane by actively pumping ions such as sodium, potassium, and chloride in and out of the cells. This membrane potential, as it was called, could be raised (inhibition) or lowered (excitation) as a result of the influence of chemical molecules secreted by neighbouring neurons, which delivered their influences via specialized junctions called synapses. The chemicals secreted from nerve endings were called neurotransmitters because they permitted cell-to-cell signalling in the brain.

When a neuron was sufficiently excited, its membrane potential could suddenly reverse its sign and the resultant differential in voltage, or action potential, could spread from the cell body over the entire surface of the neuron, including its endings, which were thereby induced to secrete their own brand of chemical neurotransmitter. The neurotransmitters that are directly responsible for neuronal excitability include glutamate (excitatory) and gamma-aminobutyric acid or GABA (inhibitory).

Most of the very successful work in cellular neurobiology was conducted under the protective umbrella of Sherrington's reflex doctrine, which provided sufficient information to help work out how neuronal circuits were organized. The reflex circuit model could explain the following: the spinal reflexes involved in posture and movement; the encoding of stimuli in sequences of action potentials in neurons, which could lead to sensation; and even the coordination of the sensory and motor systems needed to account for movement (motor) behaviour.

The reflex doctrine could not, however, help the pioneer sleep and dream scientists very much, because no link could be established between the activity of circuits of neurons (neuronal circuits) and the EEG. It had long been assumed that the EEG was the register of voltage changes in the brain (i.e. cerebral action potentials), although this could not explain the patterns of the EEG seen in sleep (e.g. spindles and slow waves), unless neuronal activity was continuous, i.e. spontaneous, as well as reflexive. Consequently, work at the cellular and EEG levels proceeded along entirely separate but parallel tracks, similar to those that Descartes thought God had used to set mind and body in perfect but independent motion. Cartesian duality dies slowly; it is still alive and well in most of us because we cannot yet see how a physical object, the brain, can have subjective experience. This is the so-called 'hard problem' of philosophy.

The basis of brain activation

Just before the middle of the last century, two classic sensorimotor physiologists, Giuseppe Moruzzi and Horace Magoun, working at Northwestern Medical School in Chicago, discovered that the experimental stimulation of the brain stem of cats could cause a shift in the EEG pattern from that of sleep to that of waking. In other words, they established an experimental basis for brain activation in sleep. Their results, published in 1949, antedated the discovery of rapid eye movement (REM) sleep by four years, and set the stage for investigating brain activation in sleep by challenging the deeply entrenched concept that all brain activation had to come from the outside world via sensory stimulation.

Indeed, Moruzzi and Magoun's hypothesis of a non-specific system that was activated by a reticular (net-like) component of the brain and that could operate independently of sensory input encountered stiff resistance. This resistance was only gradually overcome by their subsequent studies demonstrating independence of the activation from the sensory pathways. Prolonged sleep-like unresponsiveness occurred when this reticular system was damaged leaving the sensory pathways intact. These follow-up studies were being conducted just as the discovery of REM sleep was being made (again in Chicago).

How does the study of REM sleep in cats help?

In 1957, William Dement, a co-worker of Aserinsky and Kleitman, vigorously investigated the REM sleep–dream connection in humans, and discovered that cats also had periods of brain activation and REM in their sleep. This provided the experimental model necessary for investigation of the cellular and molecular basis of brain activation in sleep, and the chance to integrate phenomena at the level of cells and molecules with the EEG and the distinctive forms of mental activity in human sleep. We didn't need to know whether cats dreamed to make this integration. All we

Do animals dream?

All mammals have the same kind of brain activation during sleep as humans. Whether or not they dream is another question, which can be answered only by posing another one: Do animals have consciousness? The answer to that question has been hotly debated. Many scientists today feel that animals probably *do* have a limited form of consciousness, quite different from ours in that it lacks language and the capacity for propositional or symbolic thought.

Animals certainly can't report dreams even if they do have them. But which pet owner would doubt that his or her favourite animal friend has perception, memory, and emotion? These are three of the key aspects of consciousness, and they could be experienced whether or not an animal had verbal language as we do. When the animal's brain is activated during sleep, why not assume that the animal has some sort of perceptual, emotional, and memory experience?

In terms of the important scientific use to which we could put animal sleep in the study of human dreaming, it makes little difference what the answer to the question about animal dreams might be. All we need know, in order to learn from our animal colleagues, is that they have the same kind of brain activation in their sleep as we do. We then go on to make the fairly safe assumption that animals have the same mechanisms of brain activation in sleep as we do.

had to do was assume that the REM sleep of cats was engineered in the same way as REM sleep in humans.

The hypothesis of REM sleep correspondence across species was greatly strengthened by the subsequent finding that all but the most primitive mammals had periodic brain activation during sleep. If they had eyes, they also had REMs in their activated sleep phases. Besides shoring up the homology hypothesis, this surprising fact suggested that REM was biologically important to all mammalian life, whatever its relationship to human dreaming. Conversely, it suggested that the correlation of REM and dreaming was a very limiting way of thinking about the functional significance of brain activation in sleep.

As it turned out, both of these new ways of looking at sleep were useful and important. For example, it has become clear that REM sleep subserves body temperature regulation (thermoregulation), perhaps the most basic of all mammalian housekeeping functions. Many experiments indicate that REM also facilitates the consolidation and advancement of procedural learning. As procedural learning is the acquired ability to do things when consciousness may not be involved, the subjective experience of dreams could never suggest even this high-level functional principle. And how could we know, from our dreaming, that our capacity to regulate our own temperature was being assured by REM sleep?

Using the techniques of electrical stimulation and surgical alterations of the brain that led to Moruzzi and Magoun's concept of activation of a reticular system in the brain, the French neurophysiologist Michel Jouvet, working in Lyons from the mid-1950s onward, established once and for all that brain activation did occur and that it occurred spontaneously in sleep. He also proved that REM sleep was organized by the brain stem, including this reticular formation. By discovering the active suppression of muscle tone that invariably accompanies REM sleep,

Jouvet also helped us understand how the brain could be turned on without producing waking behaviour. As the motor system was actively blocked at the level of the spinal cord, real movement was impossible even if the upper brain elaborated and commanded the rich behaviours that we perceive in our dream scenarios.

12/3/1980 Parachute, Dream no. 29

A group of parachutists descends from behind forward – the sky is blue, the chutes white – suddenly and unexpectedly, one chutist passes the others rapidly – it is now clear that this is a contest – and the new man, from Navy, will win easily. But is his chute open? Yes. To guide his descent he climbs the cords – like a fetus shimmying up his own umbilical connection!

In this dream, I myself am not moving as I was in earlier examples, but the perceived movement of three parachutists is nevertheless dynamic and emotionally gripping. The impending doom of such dream movement is typical and suggests not only the co-activation of anxiety in the limbic brain, but also the generation of unfamiliar or intrinsically impossible movement patterns at the level of the brain stem itself, where the neurons controlling body position in space are located.

Jouvet's most radical and definitive experiments supported this idea. When he isolated the brain stem below the level of the junction of the two areas of the brain known as the pons and the midbrain and, even when he removed all of the brain above this level, he could still observe the periodic suppression of muscle tone, and occasional eye and body movements, including the rhythmic stepping that would be used in real locomotion by a normal cat during waking. In other words, one of the key formal features of human dreaming, the sense of continuous motion, may arise at the very low level of parts of the brain stem that generate motor patterns. In any case, such generators *are* present in the brain stem and *are* activated in REM.

Like Aserinsky and Kleitman, Michel Jouvet knew how to exploit the chance discoveries very well. He was trying to study something else (Pavlovian conditioning) when his cats, like Aserinsky's children, fell asleep. As he was also trying to monitor the cat's attention in waking, his neck muscle electrodes picked up the atonia (lack of tone) of REM sleep. In science, as elsewhere in life, it is an ill wind that blows no one some good! And later, luck found Jouvet ready again. As he was a neurosurgeon, studied cats, and wanted to integrate the EEG of structures such as the brain stem and the thalamus located under the cortex (subcortical structures), Jouvet was able to observe the paroxysmal (PGO) waves that arise in different areas of the brain – the pons of the brain stem reticular formation (P), the geniculate body of the thalamus (G), and the occipital cortex (O) – during REM sleep. These waves, which were markedly reduced in waking, indicated that the brain activation of REM sleep was physiologically as well as psychologically distinctive. Figure 3 shows recordings of PGO waves from the cortex, thalamus, and brain stem.

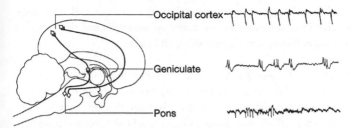

Occipital cortex

Geniculate

Pons

3. The visual brain stimulates itself in REM sleep via a mechanism reflected in EEG recordings as PGO waves. Originating in the pons (P) from the neurons that move the eyes, these signals are conducted both to the lateral geniculate (G) body in the thalamus and to the occipital cortex (O). (The three traces shown were not recorded simultaneously.)

What chemical control is there of the brain–mind states?

Although counterintuitive, the discovery of brain activation in sleep was rapidly accepted by those dream scientists who had sudden and transformative ah-ha experiences when they read about it. In the ensuing excitement about the similarities between waking and dreaming consciousness, few stopped to wonder what bit of this sleep-dependent brain activation could account for the *difference*, which, after all, is every bit as important as the similarities:

- Why is dreaming so strongly sensorimotor, a feature unmatched in even the most vivid waking fantasies?
- Why is dreaming so rarely self-reflective, when waking consciousness is so often dominated by internal thought?
- Why is dreaming so limited by impoverishment in recall? In particular, why do we lose the capacity to recount actively declarative memories (memories that are learned quickly and consciously) and gain the capacity to activate remote ones?
- Why is almost all dreaming forgotten?
- Why are dreams so bizarre?

Could physiology help us answer these questions as well? Certainly not if all we paid attention to was brain activation and the common aspects of its occurrence in waking and sleep.

To answer all these questions about the distinctive features of dream consciousness, it was necessary to know not only that the brain was switched back on in sleep, but also that this switch process was effected by quite different mechanisms from those of waking. After all, we usually don't wake up during REM and we already knew, from Jouvet's early work, part of the reason why we don't move: our muscles are actively inhibited. This guarantees the continuation of immobility and it helps us understand why we often awaken feeling paralysed in our dreams.

Moreover, we knew from the PGO wave discovery that REM sleep activation had distinct pulses. Each PGO wave, and there are something like 14,000 PGO waves per day in the cat, delivered a pulse of activation to the brain, similar to what would happen if we were startled by an unexpected stimulus during waking. This fact meant that dreaming was a mental state made up of both sustained electrical brain activation and very strong, very discrete arousal stimuli. The PGO waves could thus mediate distinctive aspects of dream mental activity such as the intense absorption (the dominance of percepts over thoughts) the bizarreness (based on discontinuity and incongruity of times, places, and people), and the constant sensorimotor content (as if the brain were compelled by the self-activation process to elaborate one movement scenario after another).

Neuromodulation and brain state

None of this explains why memory is pre-empted. Nor does it explain how PGO waves arise in REM sleep. To unlock those puzzles, we needed the key provided by the discovery of control by neurons, i.e. neuromodulation, a special kind of chemical neurotransmission by which the brain is able to change its state globally. Brain state is set by the mode of information processing: when the brain switches mode from external to internal information sources; when it switches from a store-and-remember to a don't-store-and-forget mode; and when it switches from linear–logical to a parallel associative mode. All of these mode switches can go on in small but significant ways in waking, but they become obligatory, pronounced, and fixed when the brain enters REM sleep.

We now suppose that the reason for the change in brain state is the dramatic change in neuromodulation that distinguishes REM sleep from waking. In 1960, the presence of brain stem cells containing the neuromodulators noradrenaline (norepinephrine) and serotonin were reported by the Swedish neuroanatomist Kjell Fuxe. It has since become clear that these cells change their output when animals go to sleep and most dramatically when they enter REM sleep. To summarise this story, the serotonin and noradrenaline cells that modulate the brain during waking reduce their output by half during non-REM sleep but are *shut off* completely during REM sleep. This means that the electrically reactivated brain is working without the participation of two of its chemical systems that mediate the awake state. These very systems have been strongly implicated in precisely those awake state functions (such as attention, memory, and reflective thought) that are lost in dreaming.

To understand this almost alarmingly simple hypothesis, it is important to recognize what is so special about these neuromodulatory neurons and their chemical messengers:

1. They are relatively few and relatively small.
2. They are highly localized to a few brain stem nuclei.
3. They are pacemaker cells in that they are rhythmical and spontaneous unless they are inhibited.
4. They fire at relatively low rates, in metronome-like fashion.
5. They project their fine, multiply branching processes all over the brain and spinal cord.

Vernon Mountcastle has called this unique collection of cells a 'brain-within-the-brain'. By this, he means that they constitute a mode-switching mechanism that can automatically and forcibly change the microclimate of the rest of the brain. An analogy to the temperature and climate control system situated in the cellar of a modern home, but influencing all its rooms, comes to mind.

Figure 4 shows how the neuromodulatory cells of the brain stem (area called the pons) project up to the thalamus and cortex and down to the spinal cord to mediate the EEG changes of REM sleep.

Now the emphasis on the power of the formal approach to the study of dreaming should become clear even to those who still long for the mystique of fortune-cookie dream interpretation. We can see that, when the brain self-activates in sleep, it changes its chemical self-instructions. The mind has no choice but to go along with the programme. It sees, it moves, and it feels things intensely but it does not think, remember, or focus attention very well. This, in turn, shows clearly that our so-called minds are functional states of our brains. The mind is not something else – it is not a spirit, it is not an independent entity. It *is* the self-activated brain whose capacity for subjectivity remains to be explained but whose form of subjectivity can now be understood.

This is the most radical assertion of modern dream science. Waking and dreaming are two states of consciousness, with differences that depend on chemistry. Can you digest the proposition? Or does it stick in your craw? Do you say, yes, but . . . and fill in the dots with a host of questions that are designed to express your curiosity about as-yet unexplained details, and defend yourself against the humiliation of having your dreaming reduced to a brain state? You know that *you* are more than a brain state, don't you? But how do you know that? By your subjectivity, you reply (which I haven't yet explained, have I?). So you still have a loophole, but please

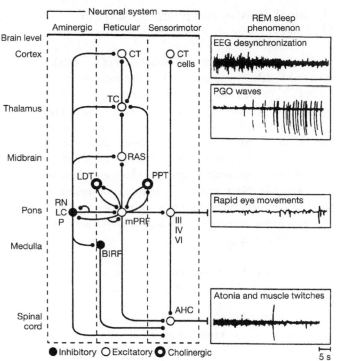

4. Schematic representation of the REM sleep generation process. A distributed network involves cells at many brain levels (left). The network is represented as comprising three neuronal systems (centre) that mediate REM sleep electrographic phenomena (right).

admit that the net is closing. And, please, bear with me as I attempt to show you how lucky you are to be such a fabulous, automatic, and reliable set of brain mechanisms that you can dream, imagine, create, and feel in your sleep. In due course, I will also try to assure you that, as being a brain does entail a subjective aspect, you are the free agent you always supposed yourself to be. You don't have much free choice but the little you do have can go a long, long way.

The biochemistry and pharmacology of REM sleep

This is a good time to review the correlation of dreaming with sleep and to drive home my point that this correlation is continuous, partial, and statistical rather than discontinuous, complete, and categorical. As the state of the brain changes continuously, it only gradually changes its mode. It does not suddenly switch from one state to another. Furthermore, the continuous and gradual modulatory changes do not affect every single neuron of the brain identically or even simultaneously. These generalizations, which all flow from neurobiological work on the state control systems of the brain stem, have far-reaching implications for a general theory of mind as well as for a specific theory of dreaming.

Mental states, such as waking and dreaming, are as many splendoured in their details as are the waking and sleeping brain. For example, perceptions may arise internally as well as externally during waking: fantasies of near hallucinatory intensity can intrude on waking and train whistles or telephone rings can invade dream plots. In the spirit of statistics, however, the probabilities of these two phenomena are reversed in waking and dreaming, and these probabilities are set by the neuromodulatory systems, Mountcastle's brain within the brain. In waking, external stimuli are far more likely to be accurately perceived than in dreaming. In dreaming, internal stimuli are far more likely to give rise to hallucinatory imagery than in waking. We need to understand the mechanisms of this contrast much better because nothing less than our sanity is at stake. Later, when we examine the impact of the neuromodulation theory on mental illness, we will see that *all* the drugs that are now used to treat psychoses have a role to play on the neuromodulators. We also see that they do so in ways that are often consonant with the role of these chemicals in shifting the balance of the brain to be awake or dreaming.

Chemical microstimulation

Once the behaviour of the serotonin- and noradrenaline-containing neurons of the brain stem had been recorded with microelectrodes and charted across the sleep cycle, it was natural to wonder what would happen if we conducted more active experiments by intentionally interfering with their natural propensities. The experimental technique called chemical microstimulation was devised, and it proved to be highly successful in studying yet another neuromodulatory system of the brain stem, the cholinergic system, so named because its effects on target neurons are mediated by acetylcholine, a molecule long known to effect movement by changing the charge of (i.e. depolarizing) muscle fibres and causing them to contract and move our limbs.

As it turned out, acetylcholine was a prime mover not only of muscles, but also of the central brain state. Acetylcholine-containing neurons fire in both waking and REM sleep, so they may help to mediate EEG activation in both states. Their excitability is apparently enhanced in REM sleep because of the decrease in inhibition from the serotonin-containing neurons, which you will remember are turned off in REM. In their variety and complexity, these neurophysiological details can become confusing. The main point to keep in mind is that in REM sleep the brain, although electrically as activated as in waking, is activated in a chemically very different way.

This conclusion was dramatically supported by chemical microstimulation experiments, which showed, unequivocally, that REM sleep could be induced by injecting very small amounts of a cholinergic drug into the area of the brain stem known as the pons. Moreover, the pattern and timing of the REM sleep-enhancing effect depended on what part of the pontine brain stem was chemically altered. If the drug was placed in a particular area of the brain (the reticular formation on either side of the midline), cats fell asleep faster, entered REM sleep sooner, and stayed in it longer than when inert chemicals were used. Much, much longer! Cats normally have spontaneous REM sleep periods that run from 4 to 10 minutes in length, and they might show 60- to 70-minute REMs when stimulated by a cholinergic drug. These chemically enhanced REM sleep periods were not only longer, but stronger, with more REMs when the drug was present.

Were we producing chemical dreams? This question is moot in cats, although even in humans, where similar effects are obtained, we would say only that we can enhance dreaming by enhancing REM sleep. As scientists, we think that all dreams are chemically mediated. So, yes, we are producing dreams chemically by helping the brain to do so.

These results have been widely replicated and accepted, which means that the brain side of dream science is now firmly established. Scientific acceptance of cholinergic REM enhancement came slowly. We had to show that a variety of cholinergic drugs could work, that they could all be blocked with anticholinergic (atropine) treatment, and that even drugs such as neostigmine, which work by blocking the normal enzymatic breakdown of acetylcholine, can enhance REMs. We can safely conclude that REM sleep dreaming is mediated by acetylcholine when noradrenaline and serotonin are at very low levels.

What all this means about the function of REMs is another question. What is the effect on learning and memory of making the brain so strongly cholinergic in REM sleep? Acetylcholine has long been implicated in learning and memory, so the REM story contributes in a significant way to an emerging picture that is consistent with our partial, statistical model of the brain as mind. Here is a sample hypothesis: we can trigger memory fragments with acetylcholine but cannot make new ones without noradrenaline and serotonin.

I said that it made a difference where the cholinergic drug was placed. When the microinjection is made in an area of the brain that is at the furthest edge of the pons (the far lateral pons), at points near to where the acetylcholine-containing neurons are found, the effects are quite different and informative; we see delayed rather than immediate REM enhancement. This is particularly surprising because the drug *does* immediately enhance PGO waves that we had previously thought might be the cause of REMs. Their dissociation in long-term enhancements of REMs proves, however, that they cannot be the cause. Besides, by temporarily uncoupling the PGO waves from REM, the delayed enhancement is prolonged, lasting 6–10 days instead of 4–6 hours after more medial injections into the reticular formation.

We ourselves are only slowly digesting these findings, which seem to point us in the direction of molecular biology rather than dream theory. This may indicate, as do other signs in the field, that the gap between REM sleep and DNA, both discovered half a century ago, may be closing. Our reasoning is as follows: the reticular site, where cholinergic stimulation produces immediate and short-lived REM enhancement, is a trigger zone; by contrast, the lateral pontine site mentioned earlier, where low immediate PGO waves and long-term REM enhancement are produced, is a control region. The difference between the two sites is that one – the control region – actually contains cholinergic neurons whereas the other, the trigger zone, does not.

Under normal circumstances, the timing and amount of REMs (and hence dreaming) are controlled by the excitability level of (among others) the cholinergic neurons. And that level is subject to a wide variety of genetic and experimental factors that contribute to long- and short-term differences in sleep, which are correlated with normal development, learning, and memory, and even mood and temperament. The brain–mind functions well if, and only if, the cholinergic system is operating within certain limits. These limits are set by biological and behavioural mechanisms that the chemical microstimulation theory of REM sleep can help us to understand.

Chapter 5
Why dream? The functions of brain activation in sleep

We have already given our answer to the question of why we dream based on physiological mechanisms: because the brain self-activates in sleep. We have already hinted that dreaming itself may be an epiphenomenon of brain self-activation, so dreaming may occur for reasons that are quite different from those that we would infer from the psychological study of REM sleep dreaming.

In the last chapter we noticed, moreover, that rapid eye movement (REM) sleep always involves intense brain self-activation, occurs in all mammalian species, and is carefully controlled by a genetically regulated chemical system. This means that, without a doubt, REM sleep is important to mammalian biology. It is highly conserved across species, quantitatively regulated within species, and varies with the stages of brain development. In this chapter, we examine the last two points by considering the changes that occur during development, and the effects of upsetting the system by making REM sleep impossible or, at least, very difficult.

Do babies dream?

The human newborn baby offers one of the best opportunities to observe REM behaviour directly. This is not only because REM occurs at sleep onset (as Eugene Aserinsky noticed in the young participants in his studies), but also because the movements associated with the pulse-like aspects of brain activation are more intense and less completely inhibited than they are in adults. Consequently, not just humans, but newborns of all species show dramatic muscle twitches of the limbs and trunk, together with highly expressive contractions of the facial muscles: as if dream emotions were being read out directly. Babies show pleasure, fear, surprise, and disgust in the facial expressions of REM sleep. Do they feel these emotions? Are these emotions the building blocks of dreams? In short, do babies dream? Our scientific answer to these rhetorical questions must be 'We don't (and can't) know'. But our personal inclination might well be 'why not?'.

The human fetus begins to show highly organized and spontaneous movement very early in its uterine life. By 30 weeks of gestation, these movement patterns within the organism include the eyes (REMs), the face (early or primordial emotion?), and the limbs (primordial locomotion?). All of these findings have profound implications for our concept of the brain–mind and how it develops. Clearly, nature has provided its most elaborate creation – the human brain–mind – with its own means of self-activation. In his recent book, *I of the Vortex*, the neurophysiologist Rodolfo Llinas has suggested that endogenous motility contributes to the fundamental sense of agency that is the essence of self-hood!

So we sleep, perchance to dream. And we dream, perforce to reactivate the brain basis of self-hood that is embedded in our built-in capacity to generate movement. Put another way, our dreams – so constantly and elaborately animated – remind us that we were born with an already huge talent for movement and for the sensorimotor perceptions of movement that become the centre of our sense of self as agents. Speculating further, we might imagine that every night, after 90 minutes and for at least two hours, we are 'born again', where that phrase, borrowed from fundamentalist

When does dreaming start?

One of the most striking findings of modern sleep research is that the immature individual, whether a human baby, a kitten, or a puppy, has a lot more brain activation in sleep than it will when it grows up. What this means is that a brain substrate for dreaming is present at birth. Whether babies have dreams is moot, just as it is with animals. The baby is developing consciousness, and has primordial perception, emotion, and memory, but he or she does not yet have language. Propositional or symbolic thought depends on language. If babies do dream, their subjective experience cannot possibly be of the same quality as that of adults.

Psychologists who have studied the development of dreaming in children find that the accounts of dreaming that are similar to those of adults start to appear at about age three, when the infant is acquiring language and propositional thought. Children's dreams then become more and more complex and interesting up until about age seven, when most of the formal adult dream characteristics are reported. Taken together with animal evidence, this suggests that brain activation is not enough to produce dreaming. The upper brain circuits that support language and propositional thought must be functional in order for dreaming to occur. The fact that human and other mammalian newborns have so much more brain activation in sleep than adults, together with the fact that the dreaming of children is relatively impoverished, also suggests that REM sleep is important for development in some ways that dreaming does not predict.

religion, has an entirely somatic (bodily) and secular meaning. If I do not yet make myself entirely clear, let me add that the formalist approach to dreaming reveals that fictitious movement – the sense of moving in dream space – is a powerful point in favour of Llinas' theory. Another point is that the only dimension of orientation that is secure in dreaming is the sense of self – I am always at the centre of the vortex that is my dream.

The following dream report is rich in bizarreness, but it also illustrates the insistent movement of the dreamer through dream space. Whether I am in the hotel, the temple, or on a Vermont hillside, I am always moving, looking, noticing, or talking.

18/6/1984 Quest, Dream no. 33

The overall theme was a quest – I was looking for something, or perhaps just a way (in both the geographical and strategic senses of the word).

One scene was in a restaurant/hotel with the usual confusion of rooms, levels, and people. It seemed like a reunion in the dining room because there were some people from Harvard there though none was identified. My job was to find the back door so as to exit directly to the street and not backtrack to the lobby. I opened several doors only to find that they were in fact windows which had been closed, by carpentered panels, from the outside. I noticed that wooden wedges had been inserted between the window frames and the panels, an elaborate contrivance for which the function was not apparent. It seemed odd that the panels would be so spaced rather than fitting flush.

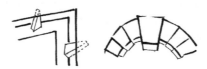

I gave up on the shortcut exit plan and started back to the lobby. Then the scene shifted to a classical temple, Greek or Egyptian. There was a narrow stair passing below a stone arch with a

prominent keystone. I remarked how one of the pleasures of working at Harvard was exposure to beauty. This seemed to explain the strange scene shift adequately.

But, abruptly, I was walking on a Vermont hillside, covered with snow, looking for an old woman. The snow was slightly off-white making me wonder if there were fresh manure just under the surface. Despite the risk, I decided to eat some snow to quench my thirst. It was tasteless.

I was then talking with someone like Marshall Newland about the old woman whom I had not yet reached. He offered an aphorism that seemed, in typical Vermont fashion, to sum up the situation:

'I may be hard to find, but when you get there, you can count on my presence.'

This seemed to mean that reliability was the reward of persistence.

The 'I' of this dream is amazingly secure given the whirling inconstancies of place and action. This report also illustrates the strange impoverishment of thinking that typifies dreams that are as animated as this one. This suggests that it is sensorimotor action, not cognition, that is important to the developmental processes that we are discussing. In other words, my sense of agency is first linked to movement; only later is it elaborated in thought.

Do fetuses dream?

In the womb (or uterus), at 30 weeks' gestation, the human fetus is spending almost 24 hours of each day in a brain-activated state that constitutes a first level of REM sleep. At birth, an unequivocal REM sleep state occupies at least half of not less than 16 hours of sleep each day. This guarantees at least eight hours of automatic, off-line brain activation each and every day. Ask yourself why? And let your answer run its full course: to develop the human brain. To make up the mind – in a word to become an increasingly effective mover and an increasingly distinctive self.

So, it probably doesn't really matter whether babies dream except in

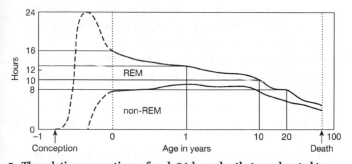

5. The relative proportions of each 24-hour day that are devoted to wake, REM sleep, and non-REM sleep change dramatically over our lifetime. Exactly how and when these states develop in early uterine existence is not known (dotted lines), but data from premature infants suggests that REM sleep is almost all of life at 26 weeks of gestation age. After 26 weeks, waking increases progressively and inexorably until death.

so far as subjectivity must develop part and parcel with movement competence, if the hypothesis of movement–agency–self is to have any credibility at all. By now, we can certainly reject as gratuitous any assumption that infantile dream content is meaningful or fulfils wishes in a psychoanalytic sense. Far from indicating psychological defensiveness, the early occurrence of motion and emotion in REM sleep argue for the opposite: a redundant, reliable, and remarkable offence designed to self-organize behaviour and tie it to subjectivity. Figure 5 illustrates the dramatic changes that occur in sleep and waking during the human life cycle.

Why do babies have so much REM sleep? What shuts the system down as development proceeds? These important questions have not yet been answered definitively because the study of sleep development is still (please pardon the expression) in its infancy. But, it is very likely that the following biological facts hold true:

1. *The brain stem*: as the seat of the most primordial (first-line) regulatory systems (temperature, cardiovascular, and respiratory to name three), the brain stem must develop earlier than the upper

brain, in particular earlier than the part of the brain housing the thalamus and cortex (thalamocortical brain) which will later support the emergence of consciousness.

2. *The cholinergic system* of the brain stem: as the mediator of internal bodily (endogenous) activation, this system must develop earlier than the serotoninergic and noradrenergic systems (i.e. systems involving the chemicals serotonin and noradrenaline), which will be needed as the individual shifts priority from sleeping to waking.

3. *Later development* of the other systems of chemicals known as aminergic systems (chemicals include histamine and dopamine) is what shuts down infant sleep and especially REM sleep, reducing it by at least 400 per cent from infancy to early adult life.

How much sleep do we need?

What happens if we do not get the sleep we need and how much do we need it? You can answer these questions for yourself just as well as I can. But, before you try, you should realize two things: the first is that sleep has now been accorded the variability inherent in all biological phenomena, i.e. short sleepers (four to six hours a day) are no more 'abnormal' or unusual than longer sleepers (eight to ten hours a day). Even if most adults sleep six to eight hours, it doesn't mean that they always do so. Sleep, like body weight, fluctuates according to the complex interaction of internal set-points, social customs, climate, and personal experience. The second is that, even when we sleep very little, we are able to compensate extremely well, especially if the stakes are high. If we are motivated – either by reward or the need to avoid disaster – we can normally manage to squeeze a little more cognitive competence out of our weary brains.

Now give your answer. My answer is that I now need eight to ten hours (and still don't feel completely refreshed). When I was younger I survived on four to six hours. As a medical house officer and sleep researcher, I sometimes went for 36 consecutive hours without any sleep whatsoever. But, whatever my baseline, I have

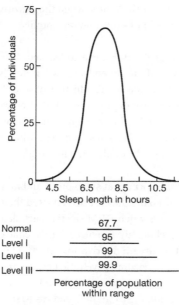

6. **Like all biological functions, sleep length varies widely. If the number of people who sleep for various durations is plotted on a graph, the result is a bell-shaped curve. Estimations of the chance of falling within 1, 2, or 3 standard deviations from the mean are shown below. Only one in a thousand people falls outside these limits, but such short or long sleepers do exist.**

always noticed that sleep curtailment compromises my ability to be attentive and to organize my own mental activity efficiently and effectively. To read, to write, to listen, and to talk well, I need a good night's sleep. And, recognizing that fact, I try my best to get it. When I was sleep deprived, and/or stressed, I was far more likely to have intense, bizarre dreams such as the one I reported earlier in this chapter (Dream no. 33, page 67).

Why have lab studies of sleep deprivation had so much difficulty achieving consensus about the costs of sleep losses and the inferred benefits of sleep gains? To understand this issue, it is helpful to go back to the early days of the 1960s, when the discovery of REM sleep unleashed a storm of experimental enquiry.

The good news is that the storm was unleashed. The bad news is that the studies were often driven by the scientifically naïve and flawed ideas of psychoanalysis. The history of so-called 'dream deprivation' is a good case in point. As REM sleep was correlated with dreaming, it tended to be equated with it. Deprive the participants in a study of REM sleep and you will deprive them of dreams. True enough, but only partially true.

As dreaming normally occurs at sleep onset and in non-REM (NREM) sleep (and no one has yet investigated the possibility that this tendency increases when REM sleep is curtailed), William Dement and his psychoanalyst–neuroscientist colleague Charles Fisher were sure that dream deprivation (REM deprivation, really) would cause people to become psychotic because they would not have the psychic escape valve that dreaming – and only dreaming – made available to them. Needless to say, some of the participants did become psychotic when their sleep deprivation was prolonged. Everyone who lived through this period remembers the stories of students who became psychotic after 10 days of REM deprivation. As a publicity stunt, the disc jockey Peter Tripp was kept awake for 72 hours in his broadcasting booth. Tripp's normal hypnomanic radio chatter was gradually replaced by fixed paranoid delusions.

In retrospect, none of these studies was morally justified because the working hypothesis was that dream deprivation would, if pushed far enough, drive the individuals crazy. Although I am disappointed with the lack of clarity that still clouds this area of science, I would not myself either submit to such treatment or expose others to it.

Sceptics such as Anthony Kales did much more careful work on this problem, and invariably showed that normal humans are surprisingly immune to sleep deprivation. When they assessed sleep deprivation's effects using quantitative psychological tests, they found no differences between selective REM sleep reduction and total sleep reduction, and only very small impairments with either. What these studies seemed to show was that there was nothing particularly special about REM sleep – or dreaming – for the maintenance of psychic equilibrium. Indirectly, these results also weakened the naïve 'hydraulic' hypothesis that it was pressure to dream that, when released, caused psychosis.

These studies did not, however, mean – as many incorrectly supposed – that sleep was without salutary effects on the mind. The idea that sleep is a waste of time is still deeply embedded in our culture, along with our commitment to achievement, doing, and material success. If you were asked to name the most accomplished American entrepreneur, you might well nominate Thomas Edison, our candidate (as inventor of the light bulb) who prided himself on his ability to be very productive on very little sleep. Thomas Edison might have been a true short sleeper, genetically endowed with a high-energy brain that allowed him to be more active, more wakeful, and more creative than most of us.

For every Edison, there is another person who will never invent anything, will never feel well rested, and should never attempt medical school. Such 'long' sleepers should take satisfaction in their sensitivity, their capacity to feel, to be, and to reflect. Poetry and literature are compatible with the stay-in-bed lifestyles of the Marcel Prousts, Samuel Taylor Coleridges, and Graham Greenes of the world. All three celebrated sleep and dreaming quite actively and began to set up a culture of internal reflection, skill in creating one's own values, and narrative production that is every bit as needed by the world as light bulbs. What, after all, are we to read when we are awake at night?

In the rest of this chapter, we see that sleep is much more than a Band-Aid for the brain–mind's cognitive competence. We see that sleep is essential to life in ways that psychology could never imagine. In Chapter 6, we learn that cognitive competence *does* suffer – mightily – from sleep loss, although this effect can be demonstrated experimentally only when tasks that demand prolonged attention and complex sequences of thought processes are used to challenge sleep-deprived individuals. Later, when discussing depression in Chapter 7, we return to sleep–mental illness connections, and realize that the same brain-stem systems that control and trigger dreaming mediate mood and mode of thinking.

Is sleep essential to life?

If we do not survive, we do not reproduce. What do we, as mammals, need to do in order to survive? We need to eat, and to convert dietary calories into fuel for bodily functions; we also need to avoid predation, especially when we are vulnerable – at night, for example. So far, so good. We need to eat without being eaten.

But we must also stay warm (or cool) enough to function effectively. This involves maintaining our core body temperature within the very narrow range of daily fluctuation (no more than 0.83 degrees Celsius, or 1.5 degrees Fahrenheit). If we become overheated, our brains do not work well – in fact they go to sleep, which is why tropical cultures are more likely to create siestas than Thomas Edisons. If we become cold, our brains are equally upset. The mountaineer's mnemonic for cold exposure says, first you fumble, then you mumble, and then you stumble, and finally, you tumble.

For us, technological kings of the beasts, 'predation' may seem like an idle threat. But think of life in the inner city and tell me how much you enjoy walking at night in ill-lit neighbourhoods. Think of the threat of infection against which we must constantly fight to avoid pneumonia (colds and sore throats are bad enough), to avoid invasion of our bloodstreams by the micro-organisms that inhabit our intestines (and normally aid digestion without asking for more than a part of our meals), and to maintain immunity to avoid invasion by a vast army of destructive viruses (such as influenza A, hepatitis B, and so on through the alphabet). These are our predators as much as lions are for zebras!

It turns out that all of these functions suffer when sleep deprivation becomes extreme. The recent experiments of Allan Rechtschaffen and his group, at the same University of Chicago where sleep and dream science began in the early 1950s, made it impossible – or at least very difficult – for one of a pair of rats to sleep. The other rat was free to sleep whenever the sleep-deprived rat was awake. In this way, it was possible to reduce sleep greatly in the one without significant reduction in the other.

It is important to emphasize the fact that these experimental conditions were so extreme that it is difficult to imagine them occurring naturally. It is also important to note that it takes two weeks, a surprisingly long time, for the most severely debilitating effects to set in. Finally, we can take some comfort from the fact that, at any stage in the proceedings, recovery is complete when sleep is allowed. We should *not* assume, however, that the results of experimental sleep deprivation of a type that we will probably never experience are irrelevant to our own concepts of sleep hygiene. Anyone who has ever noticed that even minor sleep loss leads to increased risk of infection will get this point easily.

The first defect, in what inevitably became a fatal syndrome in sleep-deprived rats, was the tendency for the skin to break down, to lose its continuity and integrity. By the end of the second week, this was associated with highly motivated heat-seeking behaviour – rats always found the warmest corner of their cage. What then ensued challenges credibility: the rats lost weight and the weight loss was so unrelenting that it could not be countered by constant eating! In other words, the caloric value of food declined, presumably as more and more of the animal's own energy resources were devoted to keeping warm. The capacity to regulate the body temperature was also lost. The very essence of mammalian adaptation – and the reflex property on which brain function depends – is temperature regulation. Without sleep, temperature regulation and normal brain function cannot be maintained. The implication, which I find irresistible, is that all of us refresh our thermoregulatory capacities every night as we sleep.

By the end of the third and fourth weeks, the sleep-deprived rats began to die off. They were metabolically starved in the presence of enough food to keep the control rat sleek, plump, and as happy as a rat can be under such circumstances. Death occurred when the sleep-deprived rats could no longer fend off infection. They were invaded by bacteria from their own bowels – eaten up by normally symbiotic hitchhikers that were no longer satisfied just to go along for the ride.

Now, you might say that we have come a long way from dreaming and even from brain activation in sleep, but I don't think so and I hope that a moment's reflection will show you why. To explain why sleep normally defends us from such fates, we must assume that it is the change in brain state, with all its chemical and electrical transformations, that keeps us healthy. A second reason, admittedly theoretical, is that our drive to sleep is so intense, so demanding, and so enduring that it *must* have important survival functions.

What about the brain activation part? What about dreams? How are dreaming and thermoregulation related to one another? My answer is that only mammals have thermoregulation and only mammals have REM sleep, so it is likely that these two functions – and dreaming – are tied together in some way. What could that 'way' be? Here we can only speculate, but before doing so let us take note of another surprising fact. It is only in REM sleep that mammals can *not* thermoregulate. We can put all of this together in a theoretical way for future experiments to investigate.

Food-finding and food ingestion all depend on waking behaviour which, in turn, depends on brain activation. In the case of waking brain activation, systems involving chemicals such as norepinephrine and seratonin (aminergic systems) operate and we know that thermoregulation depends on them. All waking functions consume energy and are risky for, although essential to, survival.

Brain activation in sleep is brought about in a very different way: the aminergic systems are turned off, so thermoregulation is impossible, although thermoregulation is not needed in REM sleep because the animal is thermally safe in its nest – safe from heat loss and predation. The brain activation of sleep is by nerve fibres that have the same effect as a chemical known as acetylcholine (and their effect is called cholinergic); it is energy-conserving and safe, but every bit as essential to survival because it allows the animal to restore the effectiveness of its core regulatory systems. At the same time, the brain–mind is off-line and free to reorganize its cognitive repertoire as well as its more basic bodily functions. We say much more about this later.

What is the function of dreaming?

It has recently been suggested by the philosopher Owen Flanagan that dreaming is an epiphenomenon (a causal occurrence or functionally insignificant phenomenon), i.e. it has no function as such. Taking this position is rather extreme, but scientifically tenable, because there is no evidence that the content of dreams has a significant influence on waking behaviour. It may help us to notice, via our dreams, that we are complex emotional creatures, but we know this already. Recall of dreaming *cannot* be all that important because there are so many individuals with little or no dream recall whatsoever who function quite nicely.

Even if the conscious experience of dreaming and its recall are epiphenomena, the brain process that underlies dreams could perform a number of functions. The most popular current theory is that the activation of the brain in sleep is necessary for us to reorder the information inside our heads, to get rid of certain obsolete memories, to update memories, and to incorporate new experiences into our memory systems. We discuss this theory in more detail in Chapter 9. In addition to this cognitive function, the activation of the brain during sleep could have a lifelong developmental role. As we have just seen, REM sleep is far more prevalent in newborn infants than it is in adults. This suggests that it is the construction of the brain itself that is one of the functions of brain activation in sleep. There is no reason for us to think that development stops once we have acquired language; we go on throughout our lives needing to reconstruct our brains and our minds.

Can the formal analysis of dreaming tell us something about how our cognitive repertoire is restored? Do we lose memory for the same reason that we lose thermoregulatory capacity – the disablement of the aminergic systems on which both depend? The net effect of resting and restoring the aminergic systems at night is to strengthen our next day's capacity for thermoregulation and acquisition of information. Along with memory and thermoregulation, we can therefore also ascribe alertness, attention, and even analytical intellect to aminergic effectiveness. In Chapter 6 we take these possibilities a step further by discussing regional brain activation.

Our dreams are emotional, and something that psychologists term 'hyperassociative', because our brains are activated by cholinergic rather than aminergic chemicals. Thus, we restore the most fundamental aspects of our cognitive capability – the capacity to order our memories in a way that serves survival. Emotional salience or relevance is a general mnemonic rule. Our level of emotional competence has a high survival value and underlies the more precise information needed to function socially. In other words, we need, first and foremost, to know when to approach, when to mate, when to be afraid, and when to run for cover. These are the skills that sleep refreshes every night of our lives by activating our brains, with no regard for the details of declarative memory (memory that is learned quickly and consciously). As with thermoregulation, and immunity to infection, our instincts to flee, fight, feed, and fornicate are crucial to survival and to procreation.

Chapter 6
Disorders of dreaming

In this chapter, we look at the way in which the brain systems mediating dreaming can become exaggerated or distorted, with unwelcome consequences. Here, we are on the edge of the medicine of sleep disorders, a topic of great interest to modern sleep science.

Nightmares and night terrors

Throughout this book, we have emphasized the important role that brain activation in sleep plays in helping us to understand human dreaming. The same rule applies to the understanding of frightening dreams and nightmares. We have already emphasized the fact that dreaming includes intense emotion, which is often negative. In fact, dreams from which we spontaneously awaken are characteristically dominated by anxiety, fear, and anger. So, in a sense, the question of what causes nightmares is the same question as what causes negative emotion in dreams. The answer is the same, too. It is brain activation and, in particular, activation of an important and ancient area called the limbic brain.

What kind of brain activation causes nightmares rather than pleasant dreams? The obvious answer is that it must be the emotion centres of the brain that mediate negative emotion that are activated in nightmares, and activation of the emotion centres that cause positive emotion determines the pleasant nature of other dreams. Having said this, it is important to distinguish, in traumatic dreams, the difference between night terrors and nightmares.

Night terrors are pure emotional experiences that occur on awakening from sleep. Typically, they are associated with non-rapid eye movement (NREM) sleep, as are the recurrent dreams of post-traumatic stress. Together with the arousal from NREM sleep, there is intense activation of the heart, the breathing rate increases, and the blood pressure may rise to extremely high levels; the person awakens drenched in sweat and terrified, and often has little dream recall whatsoever from these awakenings.

This is quite different from the more typical experience that most of us have had at one time or another – to awaken from a dream in which we were trying to escape from imaginary pursuers, absolutely terrified. In the second case, which is more likely to occur in REM sleep, we have formed the perceptual scenario of an attack situation from which we are attempting to flee, and our emotion is appropriate to the dreamed action. Figure 7 shows the activation that is not in our control (i.e. autonomic activation) which is normally associated with REM sleep. As can be seen, increases in heart rate, blood pressure, and respiratory rate can begin in NREM sleep.

In night terrors, especially post-traumatic night terrors, emotion may be the same as that experienced during waking, whether or not there is any associated dream content. The brain is activated in sleep and brain centres mediating emotion are preferentially activated in sleep as will be made clear when we discuss brain imaging data in Chapter 7. We can see, then, that nightmares, however unpleasant, are normal events in sleep, suggesting that the maintenance of these emotional systems of the brain, which ensure our survival, may be one of the functions of brain activation in sleep. Too bad we have to dream about it.

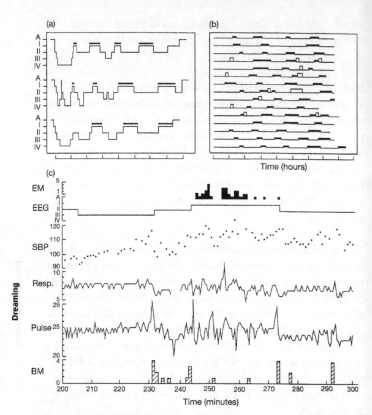

7. Sleep cycle with activation. (A, B) Ultradian sleep cycle of NREM and REM sleep shown in detailed sleep-stage graphs of 3 human subjects (A) and REM sleep periodiagrams of 15 human subjects (B). In (C) one such sleep cycle is shown to illustrate the changes in eye movements (EM), EEG, blood pressure (SBP), respiration (resp.), pulse, and body movements (BM) that are associated with REM.

Sleep walking

Sleep walking, sleep talking, and tooth grinding are three of the so-called parasomnias, movement (or motor) behaviours that occur unexpectedly during sleep. When we recall that the answer to so many of our questions has been brain activation in sleep, it will not

82

be surprising to notice that all three of these motor behaviours are a function of the activation of the movement systems in subcortical brain tissue – the motor pattern generators (or MPGs) that are referred to in Chapter 4. The motor systems that are activated are activated over and above the ability of the brain to quell motor output through inhibition.

During REM sleep, one of the most common dream experiences is of imagined motion. To ensure that we do not move, the system has to run an inhibitory, or blockade, process to stop the motor commands, which are hallucinated by us as dream movement, from resulting in actual movement. One of the ways in which the brain guarantees no movement during sleep is through inhibition; another is simply to dampen the use of the motor systems. This is well known because, to fall asleep, we have to assume postures that are immobile; we will not be able to go to sleep if we are unable to stop moving. So, the very onset of sleep is dependent on disabling the motor system. Later, when the brain is intensely activated during REM sleep, motor output has to be actively blocked.

Between these two extremes, in NREM sleep, activation of motor command centres in the brain may occur that results in behaviours such as sleep walking, sleep talking, and tooth grinding. These motor behaviours are said to be 'dissociated' because normally they occur only during waking. Now they are occurring during sleep, and the assumption has been either that an awakening has occurred or that the person is dreaming. Both are wrong. There is partial brain activation – enough to support movement, but not enough to support waking. These states are hybrids, with features of *both* sleep and waking.

To understand this apparent paradox, we need to recognize that movement is programmed by the brain at many levels. The upper level of the brain, which gives us voluntary control over movement during waking, is pretty much out of the loop during sleep. The lower brain structures, many of which are necessary for movement, may, however, be activated while the upper brain is inactive. The result is automatic movement, such as may be seen in heavily sleep-fogged individuals who need to urinate getting up and going to the bathroom or to some inappropriate place, such as the flower garden, where they attempt to urinate.

In performing such sleep-walking acts, these individuals are partially aroused, but still deeply asleep in respect of the upper brain. We know this from lab studies in which brain waves have been recorded. The high-voltage slow waves of deep sleep continue to be recorded while the individual sleep walks. One old wives' tale about sleep walking holds that it is a mistake to wake the person, usually a young person, up from such episodes. The answer to that one is to 'go ahead and try'. It is usually impossible, but don't worry about it because, if you can't do it or if you do succeed in waking them, there will be no adverse consequence whatsoever.

Post-traumatic dreams

What effect does trauma have on dreams? There are two paradoxically contradictory answers to this question: enormous impact and very little. We don't understand why, in some cases, the trauma is almost always dominant and, in others, it has such a small role to play in the shaping of dreams. One answer may be that victims of trauma, e.g. post-traumatic stress disorder patients who have had violent experiences in war, have a specific kind of awakening experience. Their sleep is interrupted by terrors akin to the night terrors of children, and, like in the night terrors of children, these do not occur in REM sleep when normal dreaming takes place. Instead, they occur in NREM sleep, the phase of sleep in which the brain is less completely activated, but in which powerful emotions can nevertheless make themselves felt.

Individuals who have had intrusive and disruptive trauma may have intrusive and disruptive emotional experiences during sleep, which create states of brain activation of their own. This encapsulation of trauma leaves intact the normal physiological process of brain activation in sleep that results in dreaming. This could help us account for the fact that many individuals who have had traumatic experiences (and I am one of them) never dream about that experience at all – it just wasn't strong enough to take on a mental life of its own and it plays very little part in the construction of my dreams.

I was assaulted on the street by three men and nearly killed by them – my nose was blasted to smithereens and my nasal septum deeply separated from my skull; I needed painful plastic surgery (without anaesthesia). But this episode has never appeared in my dreams; what appears instead are frighteningly aggressive confrontations, although these appeared before the traumatic event as well as after. This is not the least bit surprising or unusual. One of the things that we fear most is being overpowered and assaulted by criminals or bullies. That has been a part of the fear of my life ever since I was a young child, so that in my dreams I may have what appear to be recurrent episodes of confrontation with powerful enemies whom I am helpless to repulse. I run away and they chase me, and sometimes they may even catch me, as they did in the real traumatic event that occurred. But then I wake up. They never go on and break my nose in the way they did in my real life experience. In fact, I rarely experience pain in my dreams.

Careful scientific studies of survivors of the Holocaust suggest that all sleep is invaded by the horrific replay of memories of experiences. This fact, coupled with the findings of post-traumatic stress disorder in veterans of military combat, suggests that, just as waking thought tends to be dominated by preoccupations with these unpleasant experiences, so does sleep mental activity tend to be dominated by them.

We now need to carry out studies to find out if awakenings performed in REM and NREM sleep yield different reports. This is important, not only to answer the question of how trauma shapes dreaming, but also to answer questions about the function of dreaming. We still don't understand why the brain self-activates during sleep, yet evidence suggests that it is certainly not only to replay previous experience.

REM sleep behaviour disorder

The new kid on the dream disorder block is the REM sleep behaviour disorder (RBD), a very strange syndrome in which patients enact their dreams through movement. This is not sleep walking, although it *is* what sleep walking was erroneously thought to be. How does RBD come about?

The inhibition of movement or motor output, which normally quells the movement commands of dreams, is only quantitatively greater than the excitation of neurons that is the embodiment of these commands. If either inhibition declines or excitation increases, or both, movement will result.

In RBD, individuals (often middle-aged men who will go on to develop the movement disorder parkinsonism) begin to enact their dreams. One of my patients flails his arms, and hits his wife, as he dreams of driving a car and turning sharply on a curve. Another imagines that he is at a swimming pool and dives off the bed.

In every case, the dream report given by the patient on being awakened fits with the motor behaviour observed during the REM sleep dream. We know that these events occur in REM sleep from sleep lab evidence.

This sounds very much like evidence for the one-to-one theory of dream psychophysiology, proof of which eluded experimenters in the 1960s. It also suggests that REM sleep physiology can be pathologically distorted by inherent degeneration of the brain. In the case of RBD, the system controlling the neurons (neuromodulatory system) that is suspect is dopamine, a chemical neurotransmitter which has an unclear role in normal sleep.

We know that dopamine deficiency is the cause of parkinsonism and that many RBD patients will develop this condition. Beyond that, it is not clear what is going on, although it *is* clear that prolonged use of a group of antidepressants known as the selective serotonin reuptake inhibitors (SSRIs) can lead to RBD. This suggests that serotonin, which is known to be a potent inhibitor of REM, may interact with brain dopamine systems and upset the balance between inhibition and excitation of the motor systems in sleep.

Dreaming, like any other mental state, is subject to pathological deformation. In Chapters 7 and 8 we explore this theme in more detail and show how normal dreaming helps us understand the organic (physical) basis of psychopathology, the organic basis of dreaming itself, and how disorders of dreaming help us to understand both normal dreaming and psychopathology.

Chapter 7
Dreaming as delirium: sleep and mental illness

If dreaming and the psychosis of waking life are not dynamically interchangeable in the sense of Freud's model, how should we conceive of the compelling analogy that exists between them? After all, dreaming *is* a psychotic state, and it is as psychotic a state as we ever experience while awake. The internally generated perceptions have the hallucinatory power needed to make us hopelessly delusional. In the face of their detail and the powerful takeover of our minds, dream hallucinations make it impossible for us to realize that we are in the grasp of an altered state of consciousness. We are sure we are awake and believe our senses – and the associated emotions – despite the incongruities and discontinuities of dream bizarreness, which, were they to occur in waking, would immediately tip us off.

If these emotions occurred while we really were awake, our first reaction to improbable or impossible dream scenarios would be to say 'Pinch me, I must be dreaming!'. If that didn't work, we might try to wake ourselves up. Next, we might wonder if someone had slipped a mickey in our cocktail, or whether one of the drugs we were taking for high blood pressure or migraine or spastic colon had side effects that our doctor had not warned us about. For sure, we would wonder whether or not we were getting enough sleep. We would probably do all these things before we concluded that we should see a psychiatrist, although we would know that we were going crazy for some physical reason or another.

This means that, formally speaking, dreaming and severe mental illness are not only analogous but identical. This, in turn, means not only that is it easy to imagine that physical changes in brain state can produce psychosis, but also that the perfectly normal changes of sleep have very dramatic effects on our mental capacities. What's going on here?

Do we go mad each night to prevent ourselves from doing so in the day time? Or do we go mad because the brain temporarily gives up certain of its controls in order to regain them, in better order, when sleep ends? We don't yet know the answers to these questions, although the evidence suggests that each has a grain of a more complex truth hidden in this still incomplete line of enquiry.

What kind of psychosis is dreaming?

Psychosis is, by definition, a mental state characterized by hallucinations and/or delusions. It is very difficult to hallucinate without being deluded; we go into this 'seeing is believing' principle in more detail later. But, as almost everyone knows, it is quite possible to be deluded without hallucinating. Normal suspicion – call it caution if you will – leads us to believe things about our lovers, colleagues, and governments that are either completely untrue or highly exaggerated. In other words, we don't need to hear voices to be paranoid, although it certainly helps.

Which natural class of psychosis is dreaming most like: schizophrenia, major affective disorder (such as depression and mania), or an organic mental illness, e.g. delirium resulting from drugs or a high fever? If you are following my reasoning at all, you will quickly realize that the answer is organic mental illness. And, if you have any doubt, call the formal approach to your rescue.

Begin with the dream hallucinations. What sensory modalities do they use? Everyone will say 'vision' without hesitation. Although visual hallucinations are quite rare in schizophrenia and major affective disorder, they are the very hallmark of organic delirium.

Move on to the delusions: these are exclusively cognitive/intellectual and never paranoid as is typical of schizophrenia. They are rarely related to the body (i.e. somatic) as they can be in depression (a common feature of which is a mistaken conviction about lost, defective, or diseased body parts). The grandiosity and fearless elation of mania *are* shared with dream psychosis, although these features are also found in organic delirium, especially in its chronic, post-intoxication phase.

The clincher of the argument comes when we consider the cognitive deficits. When we are dreaming, times, places, and people change without warning. This orientational instability is a variation on the organic delirium theme of disorientation. Delirious patients, similar to dreamers, know only who they are, not where they are or what day it is, or even who is with them. In response to the disorientation, which is caused by the recent memory deficit, the patient with organic delirium makes up stories that are not lies but false beliefs, sincerely – and often fatuously – advanced to cover the huge holes in memory. We call this trait 'confabulation'. Confabulation is *not* a word we usually apply to dreaming, but it fits. Fabulous is a related word, which *is* often used to describe dreams.

When we elaborate dream plots, we are telling ourselves stories, fibs, white lies, and myths about ourselves. In fact, we are so convinced that these myths are about the real us that we rarely, and then only reluctantly, reach the conclusion that we are delirious when we dream. In this view, it ought to be considered at least possible that dream content is as much dross as gold, as much cognitive trash as treasure, and as much informational noise as a signal of something. This kind of proposal, which Robert McCarley and I made in our original 1977 papers about the activation–synthesis hypothesis, has never been popular.

There are, however, many other reasons to take the dreaming-as-delirium argument seriously. Even if you believe that the peculiar utterances of your aunt with Alzheimer's disease contain deep or hidden meanings, you recognize that it is her loss of brain cells that causes her to make so many of them. In fact, Alzheimer's disease, and its many degenerative ailment cousins, all affect neurons, including the aminergic and cholinergic elements that we already know to be functionally eliminated (the aminergics) or enhanced (the cholinergics) in sleep. What I am saying is that not only are the mental phenomena analogous, but also the brain mechanisms underlying them.

Sounds bad, doesn't it? Going to sleep entails the enabling of a distinctive brain activation process akin to delirium: delirium is a state that we thought we could get only by being bad or by taking drugs such as alcohol, amphetamine, or atropine, or by outliving our brains – in the senile conditions of old age. Suddenly we find out that it happens to all of us, every night of our lives, and probably more when we are being good than when we are being bad, and more when we are young than when we are old!

The good news is that all we need to do to cure ourselves of dream delirium is to wake up. This is a comforting thought in more ways than one. It means that we can stop the music if we don't like it (as therapists treating anxiety disorders and depression have discovered), but it also means that the concept of chemical balance, always so seductive and powerful, but, until now, so vague, can finally be specified. Mental state is a constantly negotiated compromise between the poles of waking sanity and dreaming madness. The following dream shows just how delirious my own mind can become when my brain is inhibited by the aminergic system and overstimulated by the cholinergic one.

28/8/1983 A House Burning, Dream no. 32

I could see the smoke, just like when the sauna and, later, the farmhouse caught fire. This time it seemed again like the house but it was in the wrong place (across the road) and when I pulled the hose toward the source of the smoke, I was oblivious that it would not reach. There was snow on the ground. I dropped the hose and ran on to find that the smoke was issuing from a chimney (at the level of the ground) hence, no danger. This house – impossible in every way – somehow fit into the familiar complex of buildings that is the farm of my dreams. There is one large barn whose repairs I frequently contemplate – it does not resemble the real barn whose repairs I also – in reality – frequently contemplate.

'Who set this fire?' I inquired angrily.

'A boy' was the answer from a man faintly resembling a scout-master or teacher and – through his expression only – implying that the 'boy' was Ian and that I should not be angry because of his handicap. He had that professional, holier-than-thou sort of patience that I myself some days evince when faced with irritated parents of troublesome children.

'He is around here somewhere.'

He was not but there was an abundance of well-meaning clinical types, a veritable workshop of do-gooders all of whom were discussing the wonders of kindness and love. This disarmed me only slightly. I was still concerned about the fire and eager to punish the fire setter.

Suddenly, there was a complete scene shift. Beside a stream, with rapid current and much white water, a ball (orange) is seen to shoot out into the maelstrom. It will certainly be lost if it reaches the waterfall. I call out to Julia, who is immobilized, at least to go to high ground so as to plot the course of the ball. (She has been playing with Karen Lavie who arrived that day with an orange ball.) Instead, she plunges into the stream and, with a manly swimmer's stroke, knifes through the current, seizes the ball, and carries it out the opposite bank. This seems, at once, miraculous and normal.

If this is not a delirious, psychotic experience, all of my psychiatric training is worthless. I have visual hallucinations, delusions, strong emotions (anger, anxiety, and elation), and, most definitely, disorientation, and its close cousin, confabulation. This story, which seems so crazy to my waking mind, seemed so normal to me in the dream.

What happens to sleep in mental illness?

What does this tell us about the chemical imbalance theory? Here again, most people can intuit the general answer. Anxiety and other emotions (such as elation) that increase brain activation of the waking type, impede sleep. They do so by increasing the set-point for the aminergic systems, which mediate waking and inhibit sleep. Besides causing insomnia, which is unpleasant, these conditions also induce sleep deprivation or, at least, sleep curtailment. And we know, from our discussions in Chapter 5, that sleep deprivation may be positively unhealthy, not just dysfunctional.

When patients are becoming psychotic, for whatever reason, sleep is also likely to suffer, adding the risk of normal dream delirium to that of a schizophrenic or affective psychotic process, because individuals can be driven into states of delirium by extreme sleep deprivation. Think of brain-washing, trance states, and the confessions of treason extracted by political, psychological, and cultural rituals. All involve sleep deprivation. In the end, sleep-deprived individuals will do or say anything in exchange for sleep.

Sleep loss is therefore common in and contributes powerfully to the development of psychosis. In the case of schizophrenia (now thought to be a disorder of excessive dopamine release and/or heightened effectiveness of dopamine), we can hypothesize an indirect but positive interaction with the other modulators of the awake state, noradrenaline and serotonin, and a direct negative interaction with acetylcholine. Significantly for my dreaming-as-delirium thesis, no distinctive changes in sleep are seen in chronic schizophrenia.

When we come to consider major affective illness, our story becomes almost unbelievably enriched. In the first place, depression, which is now thought to be mediated by serotoninergic and/or noradrenergic insufficiency, is characterized by a marked tendency for REM to occur earlier, to be more intense, and to last longer than it does in age-matched controls, or in the same patients when they get well. This means that major depression, which is also thought to be enhanced by cholinergic (acetylcholine) systems, is a functional disorder of the very same neuronal systems that control dreaming; by stretching the point a bit, it could mean further that to be prone to depression is to be prone to REM sleep and vice versa. The changes in the sleep of someone with depression, and the presumed neuromodulatory basis, are shown in Figure 8. This is a surprising conclusion because, as we have seen, dreaming is unlike depressive psychosis and depression is unlike delirium!

How can we square these apparent discrepancies? The first step is to admit that we don't know enough yet to do so. The second step is to point out the most promising avenues of investigation. One certainly arises from the fact that, although the most effective antidepressant medications suppress REM sleep (by beefing up the depressed aminergic system and toning down the hyperactive cholinergic system), they do so with quite a different time course. The disorder of REM sleep is fixed at once, whereas the mood disorder may take weeks to respond. This means that sleep and mood are linked by long-term, down-stream brain processes, which we cannot yet describe but which almost certainly depend on changes in gene expression.

Another promising lead is the immediate relief of daytime depression by a single night of REM sleep deprivation. This finding suggests that, if there is something already wrong with mood control, REM sleep chemistry induces depression. Could this induction of depression be mediated by the cholinergic overdrive of REM? Perhaps, because we know that cholinergic drugs that increase REM acutely make depression worse.

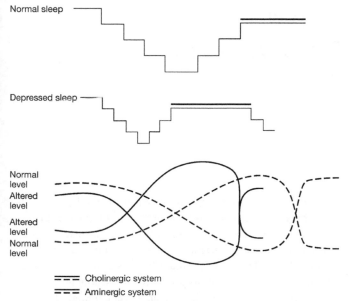

Normal sleep

Depressed sleep

Normal level
Altered level

Altered level
Normal level

=== Cholinergic system
=== Aminergic system

8. **Many depressed patients experience an earlier onset of REM during the first sleep cycle. The first REM period may also last longer and be more intense than normal. The process is reversed by antidepressant medications that strengthen the aminergic and weaken the cholinergic systems.**

We are left with the tantalizing approximation of two models – one controlling sleep, the other controlling mood – which are about to collapse into each other, but not quite. Not yet. Those yearning for a unified theory of brain and mind must exercise patience and be satisfied that, in this case at least, the cup is well over half-full, whereas only 25 years ago it was completely empty.

Chapter 8
The new neuropsychology of dreaming

Sleep lab dream research very quickly reached a point of diminishing returns. This was because the one-to-one dream content theory was too ambitious and too unscientific to guide a physiological programme that was too superficial to provide detailed data about the brain. The result was a contentious and unproductive period of sleep and dream research lasting from about 1975 to 1995. Understandably disappointed, the grant committees of the American National Institutes of Health began to cut funding for sleep labs, especially those that were engaged in descriptive, correlative work on dreaming.

During this same period, neurophysiological work on sleep in animals was proceeding apace, providing details about the brain that could only be tentatively matched with human psychology using the dream form theory. This failed to satisfy many psychologists, who were understandably nervous about the applicability to humans of cellular and molecular evidence obtained in cats, and who were unable or unwilling to give up the dream content theory. Believing that they had been unfairly deprived of support, some psychologists, led by David Foulkes, made a strong attack on physiologically oriented dream research.

Brain imaging to the rescue

In the second half of the last decade of the twentieth century, officially declared by US Congress to be the 'Decade of the Brain', brain imaging technology made it possible for the first time in human history to visualize the regional activation (and inactivation) patterns associated with changes in conscious state. Chief among these conscious state changes, and appropriately chosen as a first point of attack, were waking, sleeping, and dreaming. Although this scientific approach is still young, it is developing rapidly and has already revolutionized dream science by providing us with the opportunity to compare our formal dream versus wake measures with formal wake versus rapid eye movement (REM) sleep measures of regional brain activation.

Before describing how this method works, I show how two examples of dream formalism are explained by the brain imaging data. They are intensity of the hallucinations (which is often much exaggerated in dreaming) and directed thought (which is usually diminished or completely absent in dreaming). By going far beyond the spatial resolution of the electroencephalograph (EEG), brain imaging allows us to record the regional brain correlates of hallucination and thought. Studies using a form of imaging called positron emission tomography (PET) show an *increase* in activation of just those multimodal regions of the brain that one would expect to be activated in hallucinatory perception (the cortical areas of the parietal lobe, see Figure 9). They also show a corresponding *decrease* in the activation of an area of the brain known as the dorsolateral prefrontal cortex (see Figure 9); this brain area has been identified as the area of, or base for, working memory, self-reflection, and directed thought. In other words, in REM sleep – compared with waking – hallucination is enhanced and thinking is inspired because of the shift in regional brain activation.

How are such observations actually made? What relationship do they have to what we already know to be the global changes in brain chemistry and physiology underlying them?

If you have ever been referred for computed tomography (CT) or any of many magnetic resonance imaging (MRI) methods that have replaced X-rays in medicine and neurology, you have already enjoyed the fruits of the brain imaging revolution. Both of these techniques, and also PET, produce images of the brain itself – not just the skull – by computing density differences in the tissue (CT) or functional activation differences of the tissue (MRI and PET). This takes advantage of the fact that the density of the brain is altered by blood flow, together with activation and inactivation of neurons. Whenever neurons become more active, they require more oxygen, which is supplied by increasing blood flow to the activated region. Scans from PET and functional MRI make 'visible' such regional activations (and inactivations).

As computers are used to organize and manipulate the three-dimensional data, it is possible to look at the activity of many different brain regions, from many different angles, simultaneously. The computer, under instruction from the investigator, decides from what angle to take the image and at what depth to focus its density analysis. It then produces a myriad of pixels, or points that measure density, plots them in two dimensions as a 'slice', and colour codes the density patterns to make them easy to read qualitatively.

For research purposes, PET is attractive because it has relatively high spatial resolution. It must be realized, however, that, even with PET, we are not at the level of cells and molecules that is provided by the microelectrodes and microinjection techniques used in basic sleep research. So a gap still remains. We tolerate this gap because PET tells us things that would take decades (or centuries) to realize if we could use these microinjection techniques in humans (which we can't), and because we know that it is just a matter of time before the gap is closed in animals.

Meanwhile we rejoice at the festival of findings obtained using PET to study sleep and dreaming in humans. Table 3 shows the brain regions that are activated (and inactivated) in human REM sleep compared with waking, and compares the data with those emerging from the analysis of changes in dreaming after accidental destruction of the brain regions in question by disease, especially stroke. To aid comprehension, consult Figure 9, which shows the location of brain areas that are either hotter or cooler in REM sleep than in waking.

Table 3 Imaging of brain activation in REM sleep and the effects of brain damage on dreaming

Area of brain	PET studies on activation in REM	Brain damage studies of effects on dreaming
Pontine tegmentum	↑	–
Limbic structures	↑	↓
Visual cortex	–	–
Supramarginal gyrus	↑	↓
Dorsolateral prefrontal cortex	↓	–
Mediobasal frontal cortex	↑	↓

Key: ↑, increase; ↓, decrease; –, no change.

The following findings are of particular interest: activation of the area of the human brain known to be an important source of the chemically distinct brain activation pattern in animal REM; activation of a vast area of the limbic forebrain which is known to mediate emotion and to motivate behaviour in humans; activation of the limbic areas controlling emotion, especially fear; and activation of multimodal 'association' areas of the brain.

These regional activation data are compatible with the formalist

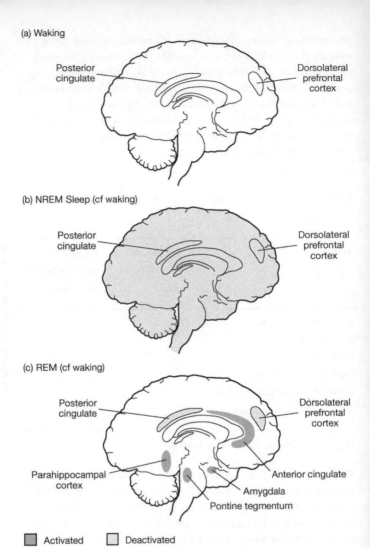

(a) Waking

Posterior cingulate

Dorsolateral prefrontal cortex

(b) NREM Sleep (cf waking)

Posterior cingulate

Dorsolateral prefrontal cortex

(c) REM (cf waking)

Posterior cingulate

Dorsolateral prefrontal cortex

Parahippocampal cortex

Anterior cingulate

Amygdala

Pontine tegmentum

Activated   Deactivated

9. Summary of PET study evidence of brain region activation in NREM and REM sleep. Compared to the blood flow distribution in waking (a), the global decreases observed in NREM sleep (b) suggest widespread deactivation consistent with the greatly diminished capacity of conscious experience early in the night. In REM sleep (c), many regions are activated about their levels in waking (solid black) while others are deactivated (shaded).

view that dreaming differs from waking in being more internally controlled, more hallucinatory, more emotional, and motivated more by instinct than in waking. In comparing the respective mind and brain forms of the two states, the dream scientist carries out a subtraction. In the first set of comparisons, we ask what parts of the brain are *more active* in REM sleep and whether they correspond to formal aspects of the mental state that are intensified in dreaming.

Dreaming is also characterized by a set of related, cognitive features that are *deficient* compared with waking, including diminished self-awareness, diminished reality testing, poor memory, defective logic, and, most strikingly, the inability to maintain directed thought. Imaging experiments now tell us that the area of the brain called the dorsolateral prefrontal cortex, which is normally activated in support of functions in waking, is deactivated in REM sleep. In other words, the subtraction in this case shows waking to have more of both the psychological traits and the underlying regional brain activation.

To see such striking correlations is almost too good to be true and, in fact, they prompt us to consider a causal hypothesis in each case. The *reason* that dreams are so perceptually intense, so instinctive and emotional, and so hyperassociative is because the brain regions supporting these functions are more active. The *reason* that we can't decide properly what state we are in, can't keep track of time, place, or person, and can't think critically or actively is because the brain regions supporting these functions are less active. Could it be that simple? Why not? Much apparent complexity melts away when science comes up with a correct simplification. This is the true meaning of reductionism.

Now we must recall that regional brain analysis of diminished psychological function in dreaming shows an association with the lack of noradrenaline and serotonin in the REM sleep-activated brain – these two chemicals are known to be necessary for attention, learning, and memory (and by implication for orientation and active reasoning). Reciprocally, we must say that the uninhibited cholinergic system (active in this state) could contribute to the positive signs mediated by the regional activation of the areas of the brain involved with hallucinosis, hyperassociation, and hyperemotionality.

The story keeps getting better and better. We might even wonder what is left for a psychology of dream content to do. In Chapter 11 we return to this issue but, for now, let us simply say that all of the features of dreaming that Freud wanted to explain with his wish-fulfilment, disguise–censorship theory are explained in just the way he hoped might ultimately be possible – by the physiology and chemistry of the brain.

Can we take our programme of integration a step further? Possibly. Suppose, for example, that the changes in regional brain activation during REM sleep in humans were somehow related to the shift in the modulation of the neurons, which could quite possibly be valid, because if blood flow is controlled by such modulators in the rest of the body, surely they should also do so in the brain. In other words, a simple way of effecting the complex pattern of regional brain activation and inactivation would be to change the balance of the modulation of neurons, so changing blood flow and then activation of the neurons. It is likely that modulators affect neuron function by both direct (synaptic) and indirect (vascular) actions. It won't be long before we get an answer from brain science.

The main point is that we can now see our own brain in action, something that I could only dream of 15 years ago.

6/7/1984 Headache, Dream no. 34

Having suffered from 'cluster' headache syndrome since January 19, 1984 – I began to notice improvement in May and June with a decrease in frequency and intensity of the attacks.
Last night, I dreamt that I was examining my own head (as at a

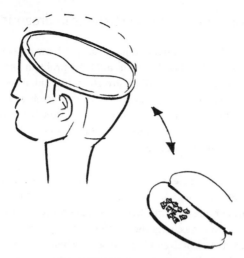

post mortem but this was not suggested in the dream). I pulled back the scalp and skull with intense curiosity, thinking 'at last, I will find out what had been causing this thing!' And, lo and behold, there was a cause – a large balloon-like mass (or was it air?) pressed the brain down into the lower third of the skull. It was concave on its surface.

When I looked closely at the left hemisphere, I noted that it was moth-eaten which explained my difficulty (almost certainly age-related) in remembering specific names. I was interested, but not frightened by what I saw; I was not the least bit aware of the paradox (tangled hierarchy?) that I was looking at my own I (= brain). For such a thing to occur there must, of course, be two brains – but then, the brain-within-the brain will suffice.

I recall saying 'Now, wake up so that you can recall this remarkable scene!'

The lucidity with which I was able to waken myself up makes this report suspect of conscious autosuggestion. But I did not, as far as I know, attempt to induce it. Instead, it simply read out my unconscious neurobiological self-analysis.

Does brain damage cause changes in dreaming?

As a result of the conceptual and political split between psychiatry and neurology caused first by the mind–body problem and deeply aggravated by Sigmund Freud's inadvertent dualism, it took dream science an inordinately long time to notice that cerebrovascular accidents (better known as strokes) and epileptic seizures (better known as fits) could cause decreases and increases in the formal features of dreams, respectively.

Strokes occur when cerebral blood vessels close (as a result of arteriosclerotic plaques) or are blocked (by emboli – small blood clots usually coming from the heart). Strokes prevent the affected brain regions from receiving the oxygen that they need to do their job. A complete loss of dreaming can occur when there is damage to tissue in the brain known as the multimodal sensory cortex (part of the parietal cortex) or to the deep frontal white matter of the brain. Table 3 shows the reader that these are among the structures selectively activated in REM sleep, which is almost certainly not a coincidence. It indicates that these two regions are necessary for dreaming to occur.

You can activate the brain in sleep in whatever way you like, but you will *not* produce the psychological experience of dreaming without activating the parietal cortex or deep frontal white matter. Why not? Are these restricted and discrete brain regions the brain's seats of dreaming? Probably not. More likely they constitute connections allowing other brain regions to communicate with one another in such a way as to sustain dream consciousness.

When strokes are centred in the visual regions of the occipital cortex – again in associative rather than in primary processing zones – patients may report dreaming without visual imagery. To understand this finding we must realize that when visual stimuli, encoded by the retina, reach the primary visual cortex some simple properties of images (such as edges or bars) are represented but the

Do blind people see in their dreams?

The answer to this question depends on whether the blindness was present at birth or acquired later in life.

People who are blind from birth have no visual imagery at any time, neither in waking nor in dreaming, and this is because their visual systems have never had the necessary interaction with the perceptual world to develop perception or the encoding of visual images. Thus, when their brains are activated during sleep, they are unable to call up images because there are no encoded images present. Naturally, vision is not the only modality in visually impaired individuals; bodily sensations or the sense of position of the body in space is markedly enhanced, and enhanced in proportion to the loss of cues given by the visual system. So these individuals do have other hallucinatory dream experiences, just in a different mode from the visual.

People with acquired blindness have had previous vision. Their brains have developed perceptual capacities and the capacity to recall the images. They can create images awake with their eyes closed and they can create elaborate images when their brains are automatically activated during sleep. In fact, dreaming is the time when people with acquired blindness see most clearly. This recalls the question of Leonardo da Vinci: 'Why does the eye see a thing more clearly in dreams than when awake?'

One of our blind participants told us that he was particularly pleased to see in his dreams because he could revisit his family at will. This suggests that individuals with acquired blindness could and should be taught to recall their dreams and even to shape their content, because they can have convincing perceptual contact with family members long after they stopped being able to see them in the wake state. Our participant was able to describe in detail the gold braid on his postmaster father's hat, which he could see when he visited his father during his dreams.

complexity of whole images (houses or people's faces) are built up and represented elsewhere. There are more than 20 such secondary or associative visual areas in the cortex.

Epilepsy is an abnormal condition in which the normal activity of affected brain regions may be enhanced as well as impaired, and so constitutes an experiment of nature that is the opposite of stroke. Ever since temporal lobe epilepsy came under experimental scrutiny – at the hands of the Montreal neurosurgeon Wilder Penfield and his neurophysiologist colleague Herbert Jasper – it was known that direct electrical stimulation of the human temporal lobe could produce 'dreamy states' not unlike those associated with spontaneous seizures.

These epileptic states were 'dreamy' precisely because they shared some formal features with normal dreams – they could be hallucinatory, hyperemotional, cognitively confused, and difficult to recall. Now that we know that the temporal lobe is selectively activated in REM sleep, we are bound to ask 'Is this just another coincidence?' The answer, again, is probably not. We need to take seriously the idea that REM sleep, which has pulse-like activity brought about by cholinergic systems, is provided with electrical stimulation to the temporal lobe; this spreads to nearby connected structures and causes us to have dreamy states similar to some aspects of epilepsy as well as to some aspects of psychosis. In both cases the mediating mechanisms are specifiably physical.

As with the imaging work, which complements almost perfectly what happens in dreaming, this aspect of neuropsychology is very new, very young, and very undeveloped. We can expect much more information as other aspects of the effects of brain damage on dreaming are investigated. What we can say unequivocally at this point is that, of course, since dreaming is a brain function, brain damage will affect it. How could it be otherwise?

Chapter 9
Dreaming, learning, and memory

The idea that dreaming is involved in the reorganization of memory has been around for at least 30 years, but only within the last five has a strong, clear line of evidence been developed. One of the most important scientists working in this area is my colleague Robert Stickgold, and it is his work that forms the backbone of this chapter.

The basic hypothesis, for which evidence was previously consistent and positive but not impressively robust, is that rapid eye movement (REM) sleep subserves consolidation of memory. This hypothesis is appealing because the brain is activated and dreams are composed of memory fragments. This hypothesis has been borne out by recent experiments, although it now appears that non-REM (NREM) sleep is equally important. More interestingly, the dream–memory plot has thickened in two important ways:

1. Thanks to progress in cognitive neuroscience, the learning and memory processes that sleep may affect have been better characterized and differentiated.
2. Thanks to progress in basic sleep neuroscience, the brain dynamics that appear to support the differentiated aspects of learning and memory are now known in enough detail to allow modelling of the sleep learning processes.

As I have constantly repeated throughout this book, we need, always, to maintain a distinction between dreaming as a conscious experience and REM or late-night NREM sleep, the physiological states of the brain underlying the conscious experience. Just as REM sleep can run without our ever remembering dreams, so – we suppose – can learning and memory reorganization take place without our ever being aware of it. The best we can hope for is that our new, formalist approach to dreaming might help us to understand the rules of memory reorganization.

REM sleep and learning in animals

Two complementary theories were adopted in the early days of studying sleep and learning in experimental animals. Rats were used for this work because cats, despite much more being known about their brains, are such poor learners. Cat owners will object to this invidious comparison – surely their beloved pets are at least as clever as rats. But cats are domesticated and don't need to learn much to survive. Rats are still wild and need to adapt to much more difficult life conditions.

In the first theory, sleep was measured after exposure to new learning, and REM sleep was found to increase as learning increased. In the second theory, REM sleep was prevented; this impaired learning. In both cases, the focus was on REM sleep. In the case of the post-exposure theory, the increase in REM sleep was often surprisingly delayed and time-limited, leading Carlisle Smith to propose the concept of a 'REM sleep window' for the consolidation of learning. This concept is akin to critical periods in development, which also involve learning, and which may also involve REM sleep because that state is so prevalent in immature animals.

As far as dreaming is concerned, the data that are most relevant to considerations of the timing of learning and of a REM sleep window in humans are the surprising delays in incorporating new location data reported by travelling dream recorders such as Michel Jouvet and the systematic lab work on the dream incorporation of experiential data by Tore Nielsen. As mentioned earlier, both sources indicate that it may take several days, even a week, for the brain to get around to using new information to change its mind. It is thus clear that, in considering behavioural repertoires, we are confronting long-term processes and we should not expect to find that all post-exposure learning takes place overnight.

How can recurrent dreams be explained?

Dreaming has remarkably consistent features from individual to individual and from night to night. We call these features formal to indicate the difference from what we call content. By formal, we mean that dreams are visual and intensely emotional, have a peculiar logical quality, and times, places, and people are infinitely plastic and changeable. In other words, dreaming is recurrently bizarre, and it is the recurrence of the bizarre features that we think determines the assumption by most people that the content is repetitive.

We know that content itself can be repetitive, especially in the case of traumatic dreams, which we discussed in Chapter 6. But when we ask normal inidviduals to produce records of the recurrent dreams they claim to have, we are impressed by the fact that what is recurrent is the formal features, e.g. anxiety may be a common element to dreams. Well, anxiety about what? Anxiety about exams, for example. That's not a bit surprising if we think that anxiety or emotion play a large part in dream construction. What things are people anxious about? They are anxious about performance and performance evaluation, and what performance evaluation is more stressful or important to people than exam performance? Consequently, we may have exam dreams as one of the recurrent themes.

Exam dreams are, however, often quite different from one another in orientational detail – they take place in different rooms and different places, and concern different subjects. What they all have in common is the dreamer's feeling that he or she is unprepared. This is not unusual in life, especially in the lives of busy, competitive people. In dreaming, it may be related to the fact that we have a great deal of difficulty vocalizing our thoughts. In other words, another formal feature of dreaming is the inability to remember. It is rare in dreams to remember something; it is strikingly peculiar that, although dreams are loaded with memory fragments, we don't stop in the middle of the dream and say, 'Hey, that reminds me of something' or remember, for example, that one of our dream characters has recently died. It is this defect in thought, added to the coupling of anxiety to one of its most common associations, the fear of failure, that may determine what an individual calls his recurrent exam dream.

It may seem to the reader that we are attempting to explain away rather than explain recurrent dreams, but this is not the case. What is recurrent are certain emotionally salient themes that depend on certain formal properties of dreams, and these are deeply repetitive. Every dream is characterized by visual perception and strong emotion, most often elation, anger, or anxiety. With these emotions come our own historical experiences – the experiences that are associated with these emotions are likely to appear in our dreams.

Human learning and memory

The distinction between learning and memory is particularly clear in the case of procedural tasks that expose individuals to sensorimotor challenges – some of which are met entirely outside our awareness.

On a task of visual discrimination – the Karni–Sagi task, for example – individuals improve their performance without knowing how or why (as they learn the task); after sleep they then do better when re-tested (again without knowing how or why). On the visual discrimination task (or VDT) individuals must fix their gaze on a symbol, an 'L' or a 'T', at the centre of the screen and then indicate when an aberrant stimulus array (\\\ instead of ///) is flashed in another part of the screen. As is usual in cognitive science, reaction time is the measure used and, within an hour of training, most individuals become very fast at this subliminal recognition.

Despite not knowing consciously how they do it, people get quite good at this task and improve markedly during training sessions. Improvement is measured by the achievement of a high percentage of correct judgements as the time of stimulus exposure is reduced. We don't think of this as memory (and it may have little or nothing to do with dreaming), but it is probably typical of most of the things that we learn and so it is quite important. In other words, we learn a myriad of procedures without being able to describe them verbally. Most learning is unconscious. We call this kind of learning procedural memory to distinguish it from episodic and semantic memory.

The next day, when they are re-tested, Karni–Sagi subjects' performance correlates strongly with how they slept. If they have been deprived of REM sleep, they behave as novices showing no advantage of their previous exposure. If they sleep deeply early in the night and/or have long REM periods late in the night, they retain their learned skill and may even improve on it. The greatest improvements occur when both deep early night (NREM) and long late-night (REM) sleep are present. As can be seen in Fig. 10, the correlation between the product of the two sleep measures and improved performance is almost one. Suitable controls, for lapsed time and for sleepiness, show that it is sleep itself that confers the benefit of skills improvement.

This result is important for several reasons: one is that it is robust; another is that it is highly replicable; a third is that, because it is

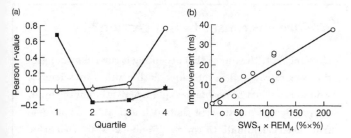

10. Visual discrimination task learning. (a) Correlation of learning with slow wave sleep (SWS) and rapid eye movement sleep (REM) across the night. For each quartile of the night, the Pearson correlation coefficient between SWS% and overnight improvement (filled squares) and between REM% and overnight improvement (open circles) was calculated. (b) Two-step model of memory consolidation. Improvement is plotted as a function of the product of the amount of SWS during the first quarter of the night and the amount of REM in the last quarter. Both amounts are quantified as percentages of the entire night. The strong correlation suggests a two-step consolidation process, including an early, SWS-dependent process and a late REM-dependent one.

entirely unconscious, it cannot be faked; a fourth is that the learning probably takes place in a restricted area of the brain that can be specified – the primary visual cortex – which makes the experimental theory amenable to study using imaging techniques. Unfortunately, it is not a task that rats can learn so we cannot easily expose the cellular neurobiology of the sleep benefits. As for cats, forget it!

Dreaming itself and learning

People who never master the Karni–Sagi task do not dream of taking the test in any way that relates to their competence. Are there waking–learning experiences that are so strong that they are in evidence within the mental state/thoughts of sleepers? We have previously alluded to the reports of skiers and sailors who notice a return of the illusion of movement of skiing or sailing at sleep onset. We also know that mental experiences at sleep onset are dream-like.

Are dreams caused by indigestion?

Certainly not. The theory that dreaming is caused by indigestion was introduced in the nineteenth century by scientists who were otherwise unable to explain activation of the brain during sleep. They thought that such activation must come from external stimuli. Of course, if one has a stomach ache, or has eaten or drunk too much, the processing of the food and resulting chemical disturbances are likely to lead to awakenings, and these awakenings may be associated with dream recall. When one is lying asleep in such states of gastrointestinal brain activation, it is not unlikely that mental content will be related to the dietary indiscretion. This might mislead us into thinking that the dreams were, in general, caused by those external stimuli.

In fact, a day's external events have very little place in the genesis of dreams. Freud thought that dreams were triggered by recent memories, but we find that recent memory enters into dreaming very little. Fragments of episodic memory of biographical events are incorporated, but whole recollections are never reproduced as such. Instead, only partial fragments of recent memories enter into dream construction and, along with other materials from remote memory, become part of scenarios created entirely from scratch as brain activation proceeds.

So, we may have to settle for sleep-onset dreaming if we want to see the effect of learning on mental content. If we are willing to accept this gift of nature, we may be able to learn from it, as our recent studies of novices learning the video games *Tetris* and *Alpine Racer* have taught us.

Individuals who are learning to play these popular games typically report intrusive game imagery at sleep onset – in other words, in sleep they still have declarative or episodic memory of their learning. This indicates, beyond the shadow of a doubt, that the brain has made a retrievable record of its experience, held it in 'memory', and replayed it later under the altered conditions of sleep. This gives us a very desirable handle and marker of waking experience that can be tracked in the brain as sleep proceeds.

Fortunately, there *is* an animal model for this phenomenon. Rats who are learning maze navigation will often show correlated firing of neuron pairs in the area of the brain known as the hippocampus, and this firing increases as they learn, as if neurons were making a physical link to represent the animal's orientational maps. The cross-correlation re-emerges at sleep onset, as if the rat's brain, like the brain of the *Tetris* or *Alpine Racer* player, was repeating in sleep the cerebral code from its daytime experience. The cellular and molecular basis of this phenomenon can now be studied.

Now brain activation in sleep can be seen in an entirely new light. It does – sometimes at least – reflect previous experience. 'Of course it does,' you say. 'I always thought that would be true.' But how could you be sure? And how could you find out exactly what was done with that day's experience by your brain without a label or a marker? Now that we have one, we are in a much stronger position to ask such questions as the following:

1. As declarative memory (memory that results from conscious awareness and associations) depends so strongly on an intact hippocampus, are our daytime experiences temporarily stored there for further processing?
2. Are bits of declarative memory, but not entire scenarios, transferred out of the hippocampus when the brain is reactivated in REM sleep?

While waiting for a more systematic answer, consider this
helicopter dream which illustrates many of the points about
memory that I am trying to make.

14/7/1977 Helicopter, Dream no. 3

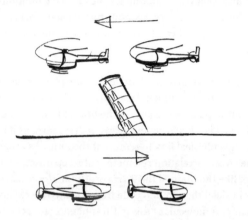

*The day I took Chris to Pisa I saw two helicopters low over the
outskirts of the city. That night, I dreamed of two helicopters going
the other way. Then they appeared to be landing in our pasture
in Vermont (Chris had suggested, the previous day, that planes
sometimes landed in high mountain Alps – which I doubted).*

*As one helicopter neared the uneven ground I noticed that the
pilot was Roger Horn (exhibit designer for Dreamstage)! I cried
out – in that silent way of dreams – to him to be careful and
suddenly, very suddenly, the helicopter became a tractor, a farm
tractor with big wheels which, on hitting the ground, flew apart, one
large wheel rolling wildly downhill while the rest of the tractor
veered to the left with Roger now running behind.*

*Like a Chaplin film, it was all very choppy and comical – but
frightening at the same time. Roger and the tractor now parted
company and I watched as Roger ran headlong into the wall of a
shed which he thumped with his noggin giving a resounding crack
and then a reeling recoil of a dazed Roger.*

With our experimental data and dream reports such as this, we are now in a position to create a new model of learning in sleep and dream memory that transcends all existing technical analysis. In the dream example given, the emotional salience (or importance) of peril, triggered by the helicopter observation, integrates two other perilous subjects: tractor operation in Vermont and my vulnerable friend, Roger. It is already clear that the brain does not store information like a tape recorder, a microfilm filing system, or even content-addressable memory – in other words, it doesn't simply take experience and lay it down somewhere in its depths for future reference.

What the brain does, instead, is to keep a rather impressive record of experience for a relatively short time, probably in the hippocampus and directly related cortical structures, which is accessible for about one week by day but inaccessible by night. This model can explain how and why I never dream of daytime experiences that are easy to recall the next day. The brain uses sleep to make bit-by-bit adjustments in its long-term repertoire of learning and memory, in a way that guarantees both efficacy and efficiency.

Take efficiency first. Suppose my brain, as Freud and many of his followers have assumed, kept a detailed record of everything. Nothing would be forgotten. There is simply not enough storage capacity for this model to hold. All the evidence is against it. And it wouldn't work very well either. How would retrieval proceed? I would need a virtually infinite look-up system that would be extremely costly in time and space as well as physically impossible. Instead, my brain reworks my memories into a much more general fabric of inclinations to act and feel in certain ways in response to certain stimulus conditions.

As far as efficacy is concerned, this is a model of procedural memory with more than a sensorimotor aspect, because it includes considerations of instinctive priority and emotional salience. It is thus the Freudian unconscious broadened and made user-friendly. No longer a cauldron of dread desire, my unconscious procedural repertoire is both rich in sources and ready to respond. I don't have to think about most of what I do. It just happens: automatically, appropriately, and adaptively. My emotional brain 'knows' that helicopters, Vermont tractors, and nervous exhibit designers have something in common.

But I *do* need a conscious declarative memory system too, and it needs to be ample, accurate, and updatable, especially around issues of orientation.

- Who am I and who are the key people in my life?
- Where am I and how do I find my way to places of importance to me?
- When did this or that prominent event happen?
- What is my current programme, and what are my goals for the future?

This is the conscious aspect of my mind and, although I want it to work as well as the unconscious does, I am willing and able to tolerate constraints and to elaborate props and tricks to make it work. For example, I use my journal to keep a record of my experience in time, my address book to keep in touch with the locations and phone numbers of key people, and my schedule book to plan the future. I simply can't remember all that stuff. I don't want to and I don't need to if I use these memory aids.

My dreams reveal how procedural and declarative memory systems intersect and interact in sleep. They always show respect for the universal aspects of my behavioural repertoire and they treat the orientational details in a relatively cavalier fashion in order to achieve efficiency – they trade precise historical accuracy for global emotional associativity. In other words, my dreams reveal how little detail of my daily experience – but how much of the emotional salience – gets mapped on to my procedural repertoire. After all, most of the details are redundant anyway. I already know who I am, who my key people are, where I live and work, and what I have done, am doing, and intend to do in the future.

Chapter 10
Dream consciousness

In his approach to dream interpretation, Freud's emphasis was on the unconscious mind, where that mental agency was viewed as a constantly threatening, barely restrained collection of socially and psychologically unacceptable desires. In turning this idea on its head, and viewing the unconscious mainly as an ally, and a guide to survival and socially sensible reproduction, we are redefining the unconscious in a way that demands a new view of consciousness in general and of dream consciousness in particular. This chapter is designed to describe how modern sleep science has contributed to the dramatic progress of the last decade in understanding the brain basis of consciousness, and how that understanding has caused us to shift our model of dreaming in the direction of altered states of consciousness that have been recognized – and celebrated – since the psychedelic era of the 1960s.

Before taking up these two themes, we need to define consciousness in a way that is compatible with the formalist approach to dreams and with the cognitive neuroscience approach to its brain basis.

Consciousness may be simply – and unarguably – defined as our awareness of the world, our bodies, and ourselves. The last quality, awareness of ourselves, includes awareness of awareness, the knowledge that we are conscious.

Consciousness is a brain function with both global and compartmental aspects. It succeeds in so far as it is a unitary state that integrates many different aspects of the brain–mind. Some of these are listed in Table 4. (See Figure 11 for physical orientation.)

Table 4 Areas of the brain dealing with the different components of consciousness

Component of consciousness	Locus in the brain
1. Sensation	Peripheral sense organs
2. Perception	Cortical and subcortical elaboration
3. Attention	Thalamocortical
4. Emotion	Limbic subcortical (amygdala)
5. Instinct	Limbic subcortical (hypothalamus)
6. Thought	Frontal cortex
7. Orientation	Parietal and frontal cortex
8. Narration	Left temporal cortex
9. Volition	Prefrontal cortex
10. Action	Spinal cord and muscles

There are two important models embedded in Table 4. One is the sequential processing model, beloved of the reflex theorists. The sequential model says that all neural information processing, including consciousness, proceeds from the outside in and from the bottom up; it passes through an integrator at the top and then proceeds down and out again. The other is the modular approach, which is used by neurologists who wish to assess mental states, cognitive neuroscientists who wish to understand parts of the mind, and dream formalists who share both the clinical goals of the neurologist and the physical approach of the scientists.

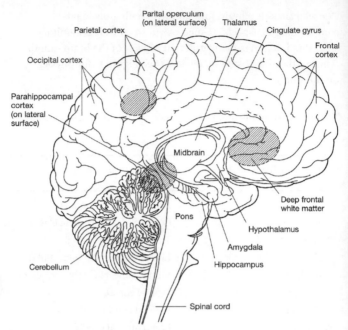

Parital operculum
(on lateral surface)
Parietal cortex
Thalamus
Cingulate gyrus
Frontal cortex
Occipital cortex
Parahippocampal cortex (on lateral surface)
Midbrain
Deep frontal white matter
Pons
Hypothalamus
Amygdala
Hippocampus
Cerebellum
Spinal cord

11. The structure of the human brain

A central problem for anyone faced with this set of modular and
sequential processes is to understand how conscious unity can be so
effortlessly achieved. At any moment, we are aware – or about to be
aware – of many information sources, and yet our conscious
experience feels very seamless, smooth, and focused. This quandary
has been called the binding problem, and theorists have approached
it in a variety of ways – by 'binding' is meant the knitting together
of disparate elements into a seamless whole. For starters, consider
the five senses that may contribute to our construction of a
perception. Most scientists assume that synchronicity of the
many brain regions contributing information to consciousness is
achieved via rhythmically harmonious activation of the many
direct connections between them. This explains, up to a point, the
unity of conscious experience, although it says nothing about how

that experience is actually achieved or how that very unity can change – as it does regularly when we dream or take certain drugs.

These normal and artificial alterations in consciousness require another quite different binding mechanism, one that chemically unites the many brain parts underlying the components of consciousness. It is my contention that such chemical unification is achieved via the influence of the chemically coded neurons of the brain stem (neuromodulation). Sleep science has shown that neuromodulation changes dramatically when our conscious state changes from waking to dreaming. The model of aminergic–cholinergic interaction thus constitutes a basis for understanding the alterations of consciousness normally experienced every day, although it also helps us understand those that may be induced by drugs, or arise unbidden in mental illness.

Binding via synchronicity occurs in milliseconds to seconds. Binding via chemical modulation occurs in minutes to hours. We need both, and we must make the best of both until we understand the mother of all questions: how does the synchronous and chemically coherent activation of brain cells result in conscious experience in the first place? How, after all, is the nervous system involved in subjective experience – what the philosophers call *qualia* – and what David Chalmers dubs 'the hard problem'? Chalmers asserts that neuroscience has not yet, and may never, solve the hard problem. If you love a mystery, and want to avoid the implications of what neuroscience is saying, you have a way out here. Neuroscientists are no more believable than anyone who waves his hands and says 'And then a miracle happens'. The brain is a colony of neurons: it *thinks* and therefore it *is*.

Qualia and the hard problem: mind and body as one

I myself believe that even the hard problem, the problem of *qualia*, and the mind–body problem itself, are effectively solved once we know that the world is represented in the brain by two reciprocal processes: the first is the a cause-and-effect mechanism of self-organization that brings us into the world, at birth, with a high degree of self-determination. This is genetically arranged. The second is our experience of the world through which we enter symbolic representations of experience into our circuits of neurons. This is achieved behaviourally.

Both of these processes, the innate and the acquired, have examples in the specific activation programmes of the brain. Viewed in this way, waking and dreaming are mirror images of one another which interact throughout our lives to create consciousness in the first place and to endow it with information for purposes of adaptation as we live out our lives.

You may feel that we are still short of explaining a mechanism for awareness or for the awareness of awareness. Think with me for a minute about how we see and, then, how we see that we see. In the case of reflexive (automatic) vision, the eye encodes various aspects of light in the firing patterns of its retina (inner layer); these signals are sent on to the brain where they are integrated as wholly abstract, but highly specific and meaningful, representations of the world (as images). So far, I suppose, no one doubts the model. If you do accept this model, however, the mind–brain problem is effectively solved. The visual world is nothing but a sequence of activation patterns of neurons representing images. It is only one step to the representation of this representation (i.e. awareness) and one more step after that to representing the awareness (i.e. awareness of awareness) and we are fully conscious. Each step involves the activation patterns of neurons.

Dream consciousness

What does dream consciousness tell us about all of this? It tells us, beyond the shadow of a doubt, that our brains are capable of an impressively rich state of consciousness without the aid of any instantaneous input from the world or output to the world. Again we know, beyond the shadow of a doubt, that the state of dream consciousness depends on brain activation in sleep – activation, including its properties of high-frequency synchronization and chemical neuromodulation, which is best provided by REM sleep, a brain state that exists before waking and upon which waking always depends. Of course, the converse is also true – at least as far as dream content is concerned. We need conscious experience in waking to represent it as such in our dreams, and we need language to give dream consciousness its narrative character and to make dream reporting possible.

What about the formal aspects of dreaming? Are we not now entitled to claim that they are innate? Built in to our brains in the womb? Already functioning, at that early stage, to provide us with the organizational structure from which full consciousness will emerge? And doesn't that at least open the door to the possibility that some components of consciousness are in place well before others? In suggesting that the sensorimotor self-activations of the brain may be forefathers of the concept of *qualia*, I follow Rodolfo Llinas, who tracks *qualia* all the way down to single neurons. Consider the following report, noting especially its movement components.

Bridge, Dream no. 7–8/1977

Last night, a terrifying bridge dream: Ian, Chris, and I are in the station wagon going up a ramp. We go off and land on a parapet – precarious but solid. I get out and go for help. This entails dropping off the parapet – some 40 feet down into water, into which I sink some 20 feet before touching bottom. Then I go up, like a shot, and try to get back in the car via a ramp. But it is one-way. Somewhere along the way, a man is lifting cars with ease.

Inspired by Llinas' bold theorizing, let us consider two related issues that are enlightened by dreaming of this sort. One is the

What is lucid dreaming?

In most dreams, we are convinced that we are awake. But, sometimes, dream events are so incredible as to make us wonder. This disbelief can be increased and converted into the recognition that we are, in fact, dreaming. By lucid dreaming, we thus mean the reacquisition during dreaming of an important aspect of waking consciousness that is usually lost, mainly the accurate recognition of the state that we are in. When we are awake, we know it and we can check on our knowledge very easily. We are able to make voluntary movements; we are able to control our thoughts; we are able, if we are sceptical, even to pinch ourselves and see that we feel things and are behaving in relation to external stimuli. In dreaming, we normally lose this self-reflective awareness; we are unaware of the state that we are in; we are unable to control our thoughts; and we are unable to make critical judgements.

During dreaming, some individuals become spontaneously aware that they are dreaming. This occurs naturally in children who are aged eight and above, and continues through adolescence. Later, it is difficult to rely on spontaneous occurrence of self-awareness during dreaming sleep. Lucidity can nevertheless be induced, and it is induced by techniques that anyone can follow. I put a notebook by my bedside along with a pen to record dream experience and then, before going to sleep, I tell myself that, being a normal human being, it is likely that I will have two hours of abso-lutely fabulous dreaming tonight. To tune in on some of it I am going to notice when bizarreness occurs. I tell myself to notice things that could never occur in waking but typically occur in dreams, namely the changes of times, places, and people (especially the unusual occurrence of unidentified characters, characters with the qualities of one person who suddenly have those of another, and so on). This fluidity of the orientation functions – time, place, and person – is what is going to tell me that I am dreaming.

When I am successful, a part of my brain–mind wakes up and I am able to notice that I am dreaming and say so to myself. Having done so, I have created a kind of dissociation: part of my brain is in the waking state and part is in the dreaming state. And then I can have a lot of fun. I can watch the dreams, I can induce awakenings so as to increase my recall, and, best of all, I can influence the dream content. I can do whatever I please; well, almost whatever. I can certainly fly and can have whatever sorts of intimate relationships I choose with my other dream characters. This is usually enough to make people quite proud and pleased to have achieved lucid dreaming.

perpetual sense of movement and the other is whether 'I' am the agent of that movement. It is I who jumps from the Dream Bridge. I drop 40 feet into the water; I go up 'like a shot'. But such dream movement is entirely virtual. It is fictitious. How can this be? We don't really move at all but are completely convinced that we are doing so. This means that Llinas is getting very warm indeed when he claims that the sense of self is embedded, at an early stage and an elemental level, in the capacity of colonies of neurons to generate movement patterns. Although this does not entirely explain how the sense of self arises, it goes a long way to solving a problem that is otherwise difficult to manage: if 'I' am not the agent of movement, who, or what, is? The environment? Sensation? A reflex? It just doesn't make sense to think that way unless you are really lazy and want God to do it all!

The one orientational anchor that is never lost in dreams is the self, the 'I' who dreams, the I who thus swims, flies, flees, makes love, fears, and fights. True, some dreamers see themselves as dream actors (rather than being the centre of the action), but the self is always there. It is the construct of constructs, the organizational unit of consciousness. I dream, therefore I am.

How does dreaming alter consciousness?

Table 5 is designed to answer this question easily. In fact, Table 5 is a summing-up of facts that you already know, although it is important to be sure that you review them and that you have one last chance to refute or refuse the formalist approach before we turn

Table 5 Alterations of consciousness in dreaming

Component	Change compared with waking
1. Sensation	Almost entirely internally generated
2. Perception	Almost entirely internally generated
3. Attention	Seized by dream events, difficult to direct
4. Emotion	Elation, anger, and anxiety exaggerated
5. Instinct	Fighting and fleeing common
6. Thought	Illogical and undirected
7. Orientation	Severely deficient for time, place, and person (except self)
8. Narration	Highly confabulatory
9. Volition	Weak
10. Action	Constant fictitious animation

to interpreting dreams. Ask yourself whether or not these claims apply to your dreams.

It is now possible to compare these brain functions with the brain regions specified in Table 4 to make our point about how these alterations are effected.

We begin by dispensing once and for all with the reflex model. The first (sensation) and last (action) are of entirely internal origin. The reason for this is twofold: first the input–output gates are closed by active inhibition; second, the central representations of sensation and movement in the cortical and subcortical brain are self-activated.

As percepts depend on sensations and voluntary movement depends on muscle tone, perception (item 2 in Table 5) and volition (item 9) are altered secondarily. In the absence of external sensations, perception is derived from the self-activation of multimodal sensory areas of the cortex and related subcortical brain areas. Recall that formal vision, like images of houses and people's faces, is the responsibility of multiple and far- flung cortical areas. Some of these are linked to subcortical systems, such as the limbic lobe for example. So we can, at last, begin to imagine how our brain conjures up dream images through the self-activation of REM sleep. We suppose that the decision to act may also be impaired by the weakening of working memory, which we discuss soon. This explains, in a summary way, four of the ten items.

Attention requires special comment. Dreams seize our attention and constantly co-opt it. We are so often surprised by the sudden turn of dream events that we cannot pay them the attention that they would command if we were awake. We assume that this attentional defect is partly a consequence of parasitic percepts arising spontaneously, but it may also spring from the lack of voluntary movement control that limits our ability to move and to think. We are awash in our own cognitive secretions, including elements of our own sensorimotor programme that are being run in rapid succession whether we like it or not. We thus suppose that attention in dreaming consciousness is weak for two reasons that are additive: one is a consequence of the disinhibition of sensorimotor programmes by aminergic systems; the other is the regional deactivation of the area of the brain called the frontal cortex.

Emotions (feelings) and instincts (primitive behaviours) are both enhanced by the activation of the limbic brain in REM sleep. In REM sleep, certain areas in the brain (namely the amygdala in the temporal lobe and the white matter of the base of the forebrain) are turned on. This is a finding on which all brain imaging studies conducted to date agree. This is Freud's 'id', and confirmation of its activation by modern neuroscience allows us affirmatively to include instinct and emotion as major instigators of dream plots. We can even agree that dream consciousness owes its often primitive character to 'release' of these brain programmes from the inhibition that holds them in check during waking. In this view, the ego/super-ego equivalents are the dorsolateral prefrontal cortex, which constitutes the 'I' that decides (in waking) whether or not to promote real-life scenarios, culminating in instinctive behaviour. In dreaming consciousness, that I is asleep (as Freud suggested). Items 4 and 5 of Tables 4 and 5 can thus be understood in neurobiological terms.

Thought (item 6) and orientation (item 7) are both impaired by disablement of the aminergic systems and regional deactivation of the global and local memory systems of the brain. We want to know more about why declarative memories, which are presumably stored in the hippocampus and then moved out to the cortex, are so seldom available to dream consciousness. Clearly, all cognitive functions that depend on memory, except possibly emotional salience, are weakened in REM sleep. Dream consciousness is therefore both a poor analyser and a poor organizer of its content. Hyperassociativity and emotional salience are the rules that govern dream consciousness, not linear logic and specific, accurate, historical detail.

Putting it all together – integrating all of these disparate elements into a credible dream plot – is the job of what's left of the executive 'I'. Here we are on thin ice because we don't really know how the dream scenarios are composed, any more than we know how ideas are generated in waking. We emphasize narration because the reports we have of dreams read like stories. This is dangerous because the reports are necessarily given in waking and rely entirely on language, whereas the dreams themselves are experienced more like films. They are multimedia events, including fictitious movement of a type not yet stimulated easily, even in the most technically sophisticated film. Only virtual reality, where the subject's own movements affect perceptions, comes close to this dream experience. Thus, we use the term 'narration' advisedly to signal the coherence of dream experience, which is all the more remarkable given the apparent chaos of REM sleep dreaming.

When we are dreaming, even without the help of the chemical unification conferred by noradrenaline and serotonin, and even without the focus and control of thought and action conferred by the part of the brain called the dorsolateral prefrontal cortex, our experience is nevertheless convincingly integral and convincingly real. Here again, it is hard to resist the idea that the ultimate reality of consciousness includes, and is strongly based upon, our brain's capacity to create a virtual reality, so close in all of its formal details to aspects of waking consciousness as to fool us, almost every time.

Chapter 11
The interpretation of dreams

As this book has proceeded, I have first knocked Freud down, then picked him up again, dusted him off, and put him back on a pedestal. But it is not the same pedestal on which I would want to place our own dream theory. How can we now summarize the similarities and differences of the views of modern neuroscience with those of Freudian psychoanalysis? My colleague Bob Stickgold puts it well when he says, 'Freud was 50 per cent right and 100 per cent wrong'. In this final chapter we unpack this paradox, hoping to make clear what speculative philosophy can and cannot do, and to show that only experimental brain science can hope to correct any picture of ourselves based on intuition alone.

In what way was Freud 50 per cent right?

Cutting to the chase, what did Freud get right? His discussion of dreams correctly emphasized their primitive emotional character. Dreams are indeed instigated by the release in sleep of primitive drive mechanisms of the brain, and these primitive drive mechanisms do include the instinctive media of sex, aggression, and escape. The feelings that go with approach behaviour (elation, joy, happiness, love), avoidance behaviour (fear, anxiety, panic), and confrontational show-down behaviour (fighting, assaulting, shooting) are also all there. This is what Freud called the 'primary process', to distinguish it from the tamer, more civilized and rationalized secondary process of waking consciousness.

But there is a lot less sex than Freud assumed and a lot more of the negative emotions than he was prepared to deal with, because he placed so much influence on dreaming as wish fulfilment.

So much for aspects of his theory that concerned dream instigation. Was there anything right about his theory of dream plot construction? Emotional salience and hyperassociativity would seem to answer this question affirmatively. In other words, we see that Freud was correct in his basic assumption that dreams are (in part) driven by instinctive force (emotions) and that these emotions are loosely connected to mental content. Certainly the one great legacy of psychoanalysis is its emphasis on the importance of feelings, so often relegated to a secondary role by rational psychologies and philosophies. Dreaming does remind us emphatically that we have very powerful instincts, emotions, and even inclinations to madness that must be held in check during waking hours.

Using this rebus (or set of rules), Freud was also correct in insisting that much more of waking consciousness than we were prepared to accept comes from our instinctive/emotional brains (or, as we would now say, our limbic systems). Moreover, we can expect to learn more about this part of ourselves by paying attention to our dreams and, perhaps, by using dreams as starting points in tracking associative trains of thought back to their imagined source in our instincts. I say 'perhaps' because this assumption has still not been proved. Even after 100 years of psychoanalytic practice, we have no empirical evidence for the power of dream content (over, say, waking fantasy or even neutral word list stimuli) to trigger associative trains of emotional salience. Indeed, as I soon insist, emotional salience is always the order of the day (or night) when it comes to associative thinking.

In what way was Freud 100 per cent wrong?

Freud's model of the unconscious was similar to Victorian sexual behaviour: the unconscious was seen as compelling, but sneaky and devious. In dreams, the unconscious wishes were always trying to disrupt consciousness, just as duplicitous sexual behaviour of waking was designed to dupe social convention. Thus, Freud's dream theory adopted the fatally flawed assumptions of disguise and censorship as the basis of dream bizarreness. The primary drive of the dream had to be expurgated or laundered and converted into the apparent nonsense of dream bizarreness. This idea that only the remembered dream content was manifest and that it concealed a dormant instinct is the very heart of psychoanalytic dream theory. Without it, there is nothing left, except the emphasis on instinct and emotion. If, as we suppose, dreams reveal rather than conceal emotion and instinct, disguise–censorship is not only unnecessary but misleading. In fact, it is downright erroneous.

Without disguise–censorship, what is there left for an interpretation of dreams using a psychoanalytically constructed theory? If the dream-inducing instincts are not disguised and not censored, but entered into the dream plots directly, then the manifest dream is the dream, is the dream, is the dream! All we need to do in this case is to record our dreams and read the reports carefully! By carefully, I mean with an eye to associations, which may be remote and obscure, but meaningful to the construction of an historically honest view of ourselves. In this view, the so-called latent dream content is nothing more or less than the vast set of associations connected to each aspect of dream content. It could still be quite useful to investigate these as a way of learning more about parts of our mind that are important to us, whether or not we think of them as dream instigators or as elements that, precisely because they are of direct and undisguised emotional salience, get used in dream construction.

Are men's and women's dreams different?

We were very surprised when we conducted a study of emotion in dreams in a group of male and female college students. We had fully expected that the emotion profiles of these two groups would be as different as they are thought to be during the waking state. We expected men's dreams to be more aggressive and more violent and women's dreams to be more affiliative and tender, but we found that this was not the case, at least in our participants. The emotion profiles in dreams of men and women were strikingly similar.

There is very little difference in the tendency for men and women to have visual imagery in their dreams, very little difference in the tendency for them to have bizarreness in their dreams, and, most strikingly of all, there is very little difference in the incidence or intensity of the emotions. What this suggests to us is that the emotional intensity of dreams is something that is a given – it is a brain-based phenomenon that is experienced similarly by both men and women.

Through their biology and social interactions, men and women learn during waking to direct their emotional energies in different ways. Women are often more concerned with child rearing and child protection, and men are more often concerned with wage earning and competitive interactions with their peers. As a result of shifts in gender, these behaviours are changing as we speak. But what apparently doesn't change very much is the representation of emotions in men's and women's dreams. Emotional salience is equally important to both sexes.

Although dream emotions are the same in men and women, they are associated with highly individual content. It is in this spirit that the interpretation of dreams – particular dreams of specific individuals – can still find a place in personal psychology and psychotherapy. In all likelihood, this is probably what has been going on in psychodynamic psychotherapy anyway.

Consider the following report of mine, which is as relevant to the physiological discussion of Chapter 4 as it is to the question of individual meaning raised here. I suppose that I am the only person in the world who could have had a dream with this content.

12/3/1980 Homage to Jouvet, Dream no. 12

I arrive at a meeting (probably the New Mexico APSS meeting in 1969) and am greeting colleagues. Suddenly I notice that Jouvet is there. He recognizes me and smiles broadly (not his usual greeting). I am about to call out to him when I suddenly lose muscle tone in my legs and sink to the floor. I cannot communicate and feel lost.

In my journal, following this report, I wrote the following comments:

- Limp legs: I first heard the French expression for this on the day that I went to a romantic rondezvous that needed to be discreet, to the Hotel de Beaux-Arts in Villefranche. When I returned to the lab, Jouvet said that I looked like I had *les jambes coupées* – an expression used to describe one who is sexually exhausted. My excuse to Jouvet for leaving the lab had been to meet my old friend D.B. at the main university library. I told Jouvet that D.B. had developed a foot fetish attachment to J.S. and that there were jokes about D.B.'s homosexuality. But there was nothing homosexual about my rendezvous at the Hotel de Beaux-Arts and Jouvet probably sensed that.
- Jouvet's smile: a beginning reconciliation after almost ten years of tension over personal and professional rivalry. Note that I had

worked in Lyons in 1963–64 and that this dream occurred in 1980. Japan (1979) was the ice-breaker. Mexico (1980) will be the clincher. Jouvet's break with Hernandez-Peon – a Mexican friend and rival – began in Lyons when I was there in 1962. Today, I received a cordial letter from Jouvet – formal, but cordial.

- Atonia: Jouvet's great discovery, the abolition of muscle tone associated with REM sleep, is represented in my dream cataplexy. Like narcoleptics in real life, strong emotion – especially surprise – produces atonia. Perhaps I now recognize Jouvet's achievement in my behaviour.

Are these interpretations valid? How can I know? Certainly, I share the psychoanalytic patient's feeling that the interpretations 'ring true'. But this is the 'tally argument' so successfully demolished by Adolf Grunbaum. The fact that these associations are meaningful to me and that they possess compelling emotional salience confers no validity on them, either as dream instigators or accurate explanations of why I dreamed this dream, or that this is what this dream *really* means!

Science demands prediction

As Douglas Hofstadter has pointed out in his brilliant book *Gödel, Escher, and Bach*, the science of dream content interpretation founders on the rock of prediction. It is simply inadequate to conduct only retrospective analysis. Everything seems clear – and convincing – in the retrospectroscope. I dreamt of Jouvet because I had just seen him. OK. There is some evidence that antecedent events may form dream crystals around which the dream story forms. And, for sure, I am concerned about his feelings towards me and well aware of his important discoveries. So this 'interpretation' (I prefer to call it a discussion) cannot be a vindication of disguise–censorship because I am consciously aware of all of the anxiety-engendering conflicts that it depicts.

Could I predict this or any other dream that I have ever had? If there really were rules governing each and every dream plot, and I really knew those rules, I ought to be able to do so. My guess is that I cannot and that you cannot. If after you have had the dream you can assign cause, your dream interpretation is subject to the post-hoc fallacy that demolished the logic of your interpretation. And mine!

Two caveats will help to make this point clear: one is the obvious failure of many, or even most, of our emotionally salient experiences to trigger dreams. As far as we know, and our knowledge is admittedly limited, there are many salient people, events, and impulses that we never dream about at all.

As an ambitious academic, I do have dreams about exam unpreparedness, credential inadequacy, and lost slides, misplaced lecture notes, being late, and the like. I call these 'incomplete arrangement' dreams and shortly offer an explanation of them.

But I never, and I mean *never*, dream of sitting at my desk, writing a paper, or reading a review critical of my grant application, even though I have those candidate dream stimuli all the time. Why don't they enter into my dreams? They are certainly emotionally salient. They concern survival, attack, defence, and all the rest. In other words, a scientific dream theory has to explain why a whole class of emotionally salient experiences cannot be a dream stimulus. Instead of these themes, I dream of related problems, which rarely, if ever, happen.

The other caveat is that the human mind is designed to see dream causality even when it could not possibly be present. How do we know this? By means of an experiment called dream splicing that was conceived by Robert Stickgold and carried out by our lab seminar group. We took 10 dream reports and cut them apart – with scissors – at the point of dramatic scene shifts in the plots. The resulting 20 dream fragments were then 'spliced'. We reassembled them so that one half were assembled as reported and the other half as hybrids, their two halves coming from different dreams in different people. There was no way in which events in the initial segment of the hybrid dreams could be causally related to events in the second segment.

Before this experiment was conducted, I was one who firmly believed that I could see meaning in the sequence of dream subplots, even across scene changes. But as soon as I tried to decide whether a given report was spliced or not, I realized that I could not tell. Nor could anyone else. Even highly trained, practising psychoanalysts failed the dream-splice detection test if a scene change was involved. This simple experiment raises many disturbing questions:

- Why are we so sure that we can understand a person by knowing his or her history?
- Why are we so sure that any text can be read with the assumption of causal continuity?

In both cases – which are common, everyday occurrences – we have the same problem as the dream interpreter. We must project causal narrative structure on to events as a matter of course. It must be a category of mind to look for, and to find, causality in nature. Fortunately for us, it is often there. That's why we have survived and that's why science has progressed despite the errors into which our tendency to project narrative causality plunges us. But, we make at least as many mistakes in assigning causality as we make correct inferences. Sometimes we are able to see this, although usually not.

Dream science

The scientific method was designed to protect us from these errors of projection. A scientific experiment is an exercise in the elucidation of cause and the best experiments unmask false causation as much as they demonstrate true causation. In so far as our new dream theory is true, we can predict that brain activation of a given chemical and regional type will always produce hallucinosis, hyperassociativity, hyperemotionality, false beliefs, and other cognitive errors. This is as far as scientific prediction can now go with dreams, but it's far enough to put the formal psychological analysis of dreams out of the reach of content analysis.

We do not dream because our unconscious wishes or drives would, if undisguised, wake us up. We dream because our brains are activated during sleep, and we do so even if our primitive drives are turned on by that activation. In fact, such drives are not concealed. Rather, they are revealed in dreams. It is the specific neurophysiological details of that activation process, not psychological defence mechanisms, that determine the distinctive nature of dream consciousness.

Dream interpretation extends beyond its own narrow borders. We are all engaged in a kind of dream interpretation all the time. Why did so and so say such and such? Why do I feel anxious when I pick up the telephone? Why do I become angry at my daughter-in-law? Our experience with the interpretation of dreams shows us that it is dangerous to assume causality and that our answers to these questions had better not be just local and narrow, and analyse only dream content.

What we need now is a set of truly general rules that help us to accept our dreams, our fears, and our rages for what they are: expressions of brain activation in sleep and in waking that have their own deep and compelling reasons for being. In the twenty-first century we will learn much, much more about these deep reasons from brain research.

Conclusion

If the question is how do we understand the mystery of dreams, the simple answer is that there is no longer any mystery – at least no mystery worthy of the creation of mystical dream theories of the past. Surely, the work of sleep science is incomplete. We still do not know enough about how the brain–mind reorganizes itself during sleep and how dreams might be used for better understanding of this function. But, clearly, we know that these details are far more likely to reveal progressive, adaptive information processing during sleep than we have previously imagined possible.

In the place of dream mystique, we aim to install dream science. And the dream science we intend to install has a solid and broad base in neurobiology. The recent development of dynamic brain imaging technology, especially magnetic resonance imaging (MRI), makes this project particularly promising. For the first time in human history, we can see the regional activity of the brain as people wake, sleep, and dream. This is a true renaissance, a genuine revolution, and a major shift in the scientific theory of the brain and mind is to be anticipated.

As I have endeavoured to point out, nothing less is at stake than a scientific theory of human consciousness. As we already know that consciousness is a brain function, and that the state of the brain determines the kind of consciousness we experience, we can begin to build a model of conscious state determination on our solid and broad base in brain science. Thus, the study of dreaming can be seen as a crucial part of a much larger project, one that will shake the foundations of philosophy, psychology, and psychiatry.

The study of dreaming is inextricably linked to the science of sleep. The science of sleep is inextricably linked to neurobiology. Thus, the science of dreaming is inextricably linked to neurobiology. So far, what have we learned about these linkages? We can summarize our progress by reviewing these important conclusions.

The first important conclusion is that dreaming, and other states of consciousness, are related to changes in the level of brain activation. Brain activation varies in a systematic manner during sleep and peaks of this function are highly correlated with dreaming. But, even the troughs of brain activation in sleep are far from the total inactivation intuited via introspection. In other words, the brain is always more active than not. Even when consciousness abates entirely, the brain is working in an impressively complex way. What is it doing? Important answers to this question are processing information, consolidating and revising memory, and learning newly acquired skills. This means that consciousness in both waking and sleep occurs only at the upper levels of brain activation, say 90–100 per cent.

The second important conclusion is that, independent of activation, the brain opens and closes its gates. But these are not the 'Gates of Horn and Ivory'. They are the gates of sensory input and motor output. Thus, as the brain self-activates in sleep, it shuts its gates so that outside information has difficulty accessing the brain. It is equally difficult for the sleep-activated brain to realize the motor acts that it generates. We experience them consciously as dream movement, but they are not, fortunately, read out as movement. What this means is that the sleep-activated dreaming brain is off-line to normally effective inputs and outputs. It is doing its own thing, as it were. In this case, that thing is the very active processing of the sensorimotor and emotional data that we are consciously aware of as dreaming.

The third and perhaps most significant conclusion is that the brain not only self-activates and isolates itself from the world, but it changes its chemical climate very radically. In particular, two of the chemical systems necessary to waking consciousness are completely shut off when the brain self-activates in sleep. Without noradrenaline and serotonin, the dreaming brain cannot do certain things such as direct its thoughts, engage in analytical problem-solving, and remember its activities. It is this difference in brain chemistry that probably determines the differences between waking and dreaming consciousness.

None of these findings was predicted by dream theorists, before discoveries started being made in the second half of the twentieth century. But they all have enormous impact on the way that we think about our conscious experience. Without such knowledge, we were groping in the dark. With it, we can begin to shine light on our most interesting human attribute – consciousness.

Conclusion

Index

A

abstraction 21
acetylcholine 61–3, 94
action 49, 121, 128–9, 132
activation—synthesis
    hypothesis 16, 43, 91
acute head trauma 20
alcohol 91
Alzheimer's disease 91
American National Institutes
    of Health 97
aminergic systems 70, 77–8,
    87, 91–3, 130
amnesia 16, 46
amphetamines 91
amygdala 130
ancient Greeks 15–16
anger 32, 81
animals 47, 51, 57, 110
    dreams 66
    learning 109
    memory 115
    neuromodulation 57
    neurophysiology 97
    REM sleep 61
anoxia 20
anti-gravitational
    hallucinations 9
antidepressant medication
    94–5
anxiety 2, 4, 8–9, 32, 93, 111
    disorders 92
    nightmares 82
    perception of peripheral
        physiology 43

approach behaviour 133
Artemidorus 15, 16
Aserinsky, Eugene 38–41, 50
Aserinsky, Eugene and
    Kleitman, Nathaniel 38,
    44, 50, 54
associationism 23, 25, 27–8,
    135
associative memory 22
associative thinking 134
atonia 54, 137, *see also* muscle
    tone
atropine 62, 91
attention 22, 24–5, 57, 121,
    130, 134
autonomic activation 82
awakenjng 10, 32
    indigestion 114
    sleep walking 86
awareness 121, 124–5

B

babies 66, 69
Berger, Adolf 36
Bible 15–6
binding problem 123
biology 44
bizarre dreams 5, 8, 11, 12, 16,
    71, 127
    Freud 27
    orientational instability 90
    PGO waves 57, 63
    repetitive 112
    sleep deprivation or stress 72
blind people 105
blood flow 101
blood pressure 81
brain activation 1, 8–10, 16, 36

Visit the
VERY SHORT
INTRODUCTIONS
Web site

www.oup.co.uk/vsi

➤ **Information** about all published titles

➤ News of **forthcoming books**

➤ **Extracts** from the books, including titles
   not yet published

➤ **Reviews** and views

➤ **Links** to other **web sites** and main
   OUP web page

➤ Information about **VSIs in translation**

➤ **Contact** the editors

➤ **Order** other **VSIs** on-line

BEAUTY
A Very Short Introduction
Roger Scruton

In this *Very Short Introduction* the renowned philosopher Roger Scruton explores the concept of beauty, asking what makes an object - either in art, in nature, or the human form - beautiful, and examining how we can compare differing judgements of beauty when it is evident all around us that our tastes vary so widely. Is there a right judgement to be made about beauty? Is it right to say there is more beauty in a classical temple than a concrete office block, more in a Rembrandt than in last year's Turner Prize winner? Forthright and thought-provoking, and as accessible as it is intellectually rigorous, this introduction to the philosophy of beauty draws conclusions that some may find controversial, but, as Scruton shows, help us to find greater sense of meaning in the beautiful objects that fill our lives.

A fascinating book, which I heartily recommend.

Brya Wilson, Readers Digest

CONSCIENCE
A VERY SHORT
INTRODUCTION
Paul Strohm

In the West conscience has been relied upon for two thousand years as a judgement that distinguishes right from wrong. It has effortlessly moved through every period division and timeline between the ancient, medieval, and modern. The Romans identified it, the early Christians appropriated it, and Reformation Protestants and loyal Catholics relied upon its advice and admonition. Today it is embraced with equal conviction by non-religious and religious alike. Considering its deep historical roots and exploring what it has meant to successive generations, Paul Strohm highlights why this particularly European concept deserves its reputation as 'one of the prouder Western contributions to human rights and human dignity throughout the world.

www.oup.com/vsi

FORENSIC PSYCHOLOGY
A Very Short Introduction
David Canter

Lie detection, offender profiling, jury selection, insanity in
the law, predicting the risk of re-offending, the minds of serial
killers and many other topics that fill news and fiction are all
aspects of the rapidly developing area of scientific psychology
broadly known as Forensic Psychology. *Forensic Psychology:
A Very Short Introduction* discusses all the aspects of psychology
that are relevant to the legal and criminal process as a whole.
It includes explanations of criminal behaviour and criminality,
including the role of mental disorder in crime, and discusses
how forensic psychology contributes to helping investigate
the crime and catching the perpetrators.

www.oup.com/vsi

GENIUS
A Very Short Introduction
Andrew Robinson

Genius is highly individual and unique, of course, yet it shares a compelling, inevitable quality for professionals and the general public alike. Darwin's ideas are still required reading for every working biologist; they continue to generate fresh thinking and experiments around the world. So do Einstein's theories among physicists. Shakespeare's plays and Mozart's melodies and harmonies continue to move people in languages and cultures far removed from their native England and Austria. Contemporary 'geniuses' may come and go, but the idea of genius will not let go of us. Genius is the name we give to a quality of work that transcends fashion, celebrity, fame, and reputation: the opposite of a period piece. Somehow, genius abolishes both the time and the place of its origin.

www.oup.com/vsi

ONLINE
CATALOGUE
A Very Short Introduction

Our online catalogue is designed to make it easy to find your
ideal Very Short Introduction. View the entire collection by subject
area, watch author videos, read sample chapters, and download
reading guides.

http://fds.oup.com/www.oup.co.uk/general/vsi/index.html

SOCIAL MEDIA
Very Short Introduction

Join our community

www.oup.com/vsi

- Join us online at the official Very Short Introductions **Facebook** page.
- Access the thoughts and musings of our authors with our online **blog**.
- Sign up for our monthly **e-newsletter** to receive information on all new titles publishing that month.
- Browse the full range of Very Short Introductions online.
- Read **extracts** from the Introductions for free.
- Visit our library of **Reading Guides**. These guides, written by our expert authors will help you to question again, why you think what you think.
- If you are a teacher or lecturer you can order inspection copies quickly and simply via our website.